A TASTE OF THE TOUR™

FROM

THE TOUR WIVES ASSOCIATION

AND

CREDITS

A TASTE OF THE TOUR™

Copyright © 2000 TOUR Wives Association, Inc.

TOM CARPENTER
Director of Book Development

JENNIFER GUINEA
Book Development Coordinator

SHARI GROSS
LAURA BELPEDIO
Book Development Assistants

PEGGY LAURITSEN DESIGN GROUP
Book Design and Production

PHIL AARRESTAD
Commissioned Photography

ROBIN KRAUSE
Food Stylist

SPECIAL THANKS TO:
Sara Moores, PGA TOUR; Lauren McGovern, TOUR Wives Association; Jennifer McCarron, TOUR Wives Association; PGA Tour Wives, Players and Staff; PGA TOUR Photo Services; PGA TOUR Partners Club.

10 9 8 7 6 5 4 3 2 1
ISBN 0-9714428-0-0

Zucchini Bread
BREADS & MUFFINS
page 39

Jan Smuts' Tea Cakes
DESSERTS
page 135

Chicken Pot Pie
POULTRY
page 55

ABOUT THE TOUR WIVES ASSCOCIATION

he TOUR Wives Association is a Florida non-profit organization that provides assistance to needy children and their families throughout the country. Started in 1988, its 121 members are the wives of professional golfers on the PGA TOUR, the BUY.COM TOUR and others who support their charitable endeavors. By organizing and promoting fundraising events, the TOUR Wives Association has been able to donate over $1.5 million to children's charities across the United States.

The TOUR Wives Association wishes to thank the many individuals who have worked over the years to bring *A Taste of the TOUR* together. Sara Moores at PGA TOUR headquarters has helped keep this project alive for almost a decade. Cathi Triplett, Patti Inman, Cissye Gallagher, Lauren McGovern and Lisa Cink are a few of the wives who have begged, borrowed and coerced recipes to make this book possible! Although the membership of the Association varies from year to year, the commitment of the entire group to this and other fundraising projects has made a difference in the lives of needy children.

Thanks are also extended to Viking Range Corp of Greenwood, Mississippi, who generously donated a Viking refrigerator for our "cookbook naming" contest. And a heartfelt thanks to the PGA TOUR for supporting our organization throughout the years and for showing us that giving back to the local communities is just as rewarding and fun as the game of golf.

Lastly, we would like to pay a special remembrance to Winnie Palmer and Rene Appleby, who were friends and supporters of the TOUR Wives Association and who will be greatly missed by all.

© PGA TOUR Photo Services

Taste of the TOUR fundraising event, Houston, TX

© PGA TOUR Photo Services

Target House playground, Memphis, TN, donated by the TOUR Wives Association

INTRODUCTION

COME ALONG ON A TASTE OF THE TOUR!

Playing golf on the PGA TOUR, any tour, is hard work. Sure, there's some glamour involved, and earning your living on the golf course can't be all bad. But think of the days and weeks and months on the road, all the meals out, a different bed every week ... it's easy to forget that TOUR players are family men too — guys who love their wives and kids, but have precious little time at home.

Even if the family goes on the road too once in awhile, one comfort that can't always be replaced is good, home-cooked food. Something as simple as that becomes very special when you can't get it every day. As the pages to come will show you, TOUR players have some good food waiting for them when they get home!

So here are their favorite recipes — straight from TOUR wives, mothers and mothers-in-law ... even a few players you'll recognize. In the end, your family is not that different from a TOUR family, and can appreciate good recipes. So, sort of like squeezing in nine holes of golf before dinner, we've managed to pack it all in — over 200 recipes — in the nine chapters that follow.

Appetizers, soups & salads, breads & muffins, poultry and meat dishes, seafood, vegetables & casseroles, rice & pasta dishes and desserts ... you'll find ideas from the informal and casual to those suitable for your most favored guests.

We're glad to be sharing this *Taste of the TOUR* with you. Here are our best wishes for good golfing, a happy and healthy family ... and good eating too!

Arizona Guacamole, page 16

Phoenix Open Pasta, page 104

Pork Tenderloin with Bourbon Marinade, page 63

APPETIZERS

CHEDDAR CHEESE PUFFS

JENNIFER (TOM) SCHERRER

2 cups (8 oz.) shredded cheddar cheese
$1/2$ cup butter, softened
1 cup all-purpose flour
48 small pimiento-stuffed olives

Heat oven to 400°F.

In small bowl, combine cheese and butter; mix well. Add flour; mix well with hands. Shape 1 teaspoon cheese mixture around each olive, covering completely.

Place olives on ungreased baking sheet. Bake 15 minutes. Serve hot.

SLOW COOKER DIP

RYNDEE (MICHAEL) CLARK

This recipe was passed on to me from Mike's mother. This dip has been one of his favorites for years.

1 lb. ground beef
1 lb. sausage
1 (1-lb.) loaf processed cheese spread, cubed
1 ($10^3/4$-oz.) can cream of chicken soup
1 ($10^3/4$-oz.) can cream of mushroom soup
2 oz. jalapeño chiles

In large skillet, cook ground beef and sausage over medium-high heat until well browned; drain thoroughly. Stir in cheese, soups and chiles; mix well.

Transfer mixture to slow cooker. Cook on low setting 1 hour, stirring occasionally. Serve warm with tortilla chips.

VEGGIE DIP

JENNI HOEFFEL AND
DEBBYE (BRIAN) WATTS

This is a wonderful appetizer dip. It is something easy for Brian and I to take to any party or gathering.

1 (8-oz.) pkg. cream cheese, softened
1 (10-oz.) pkg. frozen chopped spinach, thawed, squeezed dry
$1/3$ cup salsa
$1/3$ cup chopped green onions
$1/3$ cup chopped plum tomatoes
$1/3$ cup chopped green bell pepper
$1/4$ teaspoon ground cumin

In small bowl, combine cream cheese, spinach, salsa, onions, tomatoes, bell pepper and cumin; mix until well blended. Refrigerate, covered, 1 to 2 hours or until chilled.

Before serving, in microwave-safe bowl, cook dip on high $1 1/2$ to 2 minutes or until hot. Serve with tortilla chips, if desired.

GINGER FRUIT DIP

SUE (JOEY) SINDELAR

1 (3.4-oz.) pkg. instant vanilla pudding mix
$1 1/2$ cups milk
1 (6-oz.) can frozen orange juice concentrate, thawed
$1/4$ cup sour cream
$1/4$ teaspoon ground ginger

In medium bowl, combine pudding mix, milk and orange juice concentrate; beat at high speed 1 minute. Stir in sour cream and ginger; mix well. Refrigerate overnight. Serve with fresh fruit.

GINGER FRUIT DIP

COCKTAIL MEATBALLS

DEBBYE (BRIAN) WATTS

1 lb. ground beef
1/2 cup dry bread crumbs
1/3 cup chopped onion
1/4 cup milk
1 egg
1 tablespoon chopped fresh parsley
1 teaspoon salt
1/8 teaspoon freshly ground pepper
1/2 teaspoon Worcestershire sauce
1 (12-oz.) bottle chili sauce
1 (10-oz.) jar grape jelly

Heat oven to 350°F.

In medium bowl, combine ground beef, bread crumbs, onion, milk, egg, parsley, salt, pepper and Worcestershire sauce; mix until well blended. Shape mixture into 1-inch balls. Place meatballs in ungreased 13x9-inch pan. Bake 30 minutes. Drain on paper towels.

Meanwhile, heat chili sauce and jelly in medium saucepan over medium-high heat, stirring constantly, until jelly is melted. Add meatballs; stir until completely coated. Simmer, uncovered, 30 minutes.

SAUSAGE BALLS

SUE (BRAD) BRYANT
This is a great appetizer that Brad and I use to tide over the munchies while finishing the preparations for Christmas or Thanksgiving dinner.

1 lb. bulk sausage, cooked, drained
4 cups (16 oz.) shredded sharp cheddar cheese
2 cups baking mix

Heat oven to 350°F.

In large bowl, combine sausage, cheese and baking mix; mix with your hands until well blended. Roll mixture into 7 (1-inch) balls; place in 3-quart casserole. Bake 20 minutes or until sausage is no longer pink in center.

ARTICHOKE DIP

LAUREN (JIM) McGOVERN
It just doesn't get any easier than this! Jimmy and I often entertain last minute and this dish is great because it only takes a few minutes to make and is always a crowd pleaser.

1 (14-oz.) can artichoke hearts, drained
1 cup mayonnaise
1 cup (4 oz.) plus 1 tablespoon freshly grated
   Parmesan cheese

Heat oven to 350°F.

Coarsely chop artichokes. In small bowl, combine mayonnaise and 1 cup of the cheese; mix until well combined.

Spread mixture in ungreased 11x7-inch baking dish. Bake 25 minutes or until light golden brown. Sprinkle with remaining 1 tablespoon cheese. Serve with crackers or bread, if desired.

GUACAMOLE

LAURA (JOHN) FLANNERY
John and I like to use this recipe when we have tacos and Layered Mexican Bean Dip (page 16). It is a great combination.

1 avocado
1 tablespoon mayonnaise
2 tablespoons salsa
1/2 teaspon lemon-pepper seasoning
1 teaspoon garlic powder
1/2 teaspoon fresh lemon juice

In large bowl, mash avocado. Add mayonnaise, salsa, lemon pepper, garlic powder and lemon juice; mix well. Serve immediately.

SUN-DRIED TOMATOES TAPENADE

KAREN (BRANDEL) CHAMBLEE

This is a simple and tasty appetizer to prepare. It has become quite a popular dish to serve when Brandel and I have friends over. For variety, serve Tapenade in sliced fresh eggplant.

1/4 cup chopped sun-dried tomatoes
1/4 cup chopped ripe olives
1/4 cup chopped green olives
2 tablespoons olive oil
1/4 cup balsamic vinegar
1/8 teaspoon freshly ground pepper
1 tablespoon chopped fresh basil
Fresh parsley
1 loaf fresh baguette, cut into 1/2-inch slices
1/2 cup (2 oz.) freshly grated Parmesan cheese

In medium bowl, combine tomatoes and olives; mix well. Add oil, vinegar, pepper, basil and parsley; mix gently. Refrigerate, covered, 1 to 2 hours or until chilled.

Heat broiler. Place baguette slices on ungreased baking sheet; broil 1 to 2 minutes or until light brown. Turn over. Spread each slice with 2 teaspoons tomato mixture; top with 1/2 to 1 teaspoon cheese. Broil an additional 1 to 2 minutes or until cheese is melted.

Sun-Dried Tomatoes Tapenade

SPIEDINI

CATHI (KIRK) TRIPLETT

This recipe is mimicked from one tried at an authentic Italian restaurant in New York City. Kirk and I would eat there every night of the Buick Classic if it weren't so far from Westchester.

1 to 2 tablespoons marinara or tomato sauce
1/2 cup consommé
1/2 cup white wine
1 tablespoon butter
1 tablespoon fresh lemon juice
1 1/2 cups egg wash
2 cups all-purpose flour
1 (8-oz.) pkg. shredded mozzarella cheese
2 slices white bread, crusts removed
Vegetable oil

In large skillet, combine marinara sauce, consommé, wine, butter and lemon juice. Cook over medium-high heat until reduced and thickened. Spoon into microwave-safe bowl. Set aside.

Pour egg wash into small bowl; set aside. Pour flour into another small bowl; set aside.

Cut cheese 1 inch thick. Place cheese slice between slices of bread. Cut bread into quarters diagonally; making triangles. Insert toothpick into center of each triangle.

Dip each triangle in egg wash, then in flour. In fryer, heat oil to 350°F. Fry triangles until golden brown.

To serve, remove toothpicks from spiedini and place on microwave-safe serving platter. Transfer spiedini and marinara mixture to microwave; heat on High 4 to 5 minutes or until hot.

CRAB DIP

SALLY (HALE) IRWIN

1 lb. cooked crabmeat
1 cup mayonnaise
1/2 cup (2 oz.) finely shredded cheddar cheese
2 green onions, chopped
Dash curry powder

In large bowl, combine crabmeat, mayonnaise, cheese, onions and curry powder; mix well. Refrigerate 1 hour. Serve with crackers, if desired.

HOT CRAB DIP

K.C. (ROBIN) FREEMAN

2 (8-oz.) pkg. cream cheese
2 (6-oz.) cans crabmeat
1 garlic clove, minced
1/4 cup mayonnaise
2 teaspoons mustard
1/4 cup sherry

In large saucepan, combine cream cheese, crabmeat, garlic, mayonnaise, mustard and sherry; heat over medium heat until bubbly. Serve with crackers or chips, if desired.

NACHOS CASSEROLE

MARIA (RAYMOND) FLOYD

1/2 lb. lean ground beef
1/2 lb. chorizo or hot Italian sausage
1 large onion, finely chopped
1/2 teaspoon hot pepper sauce
1/4 teaspoon salt
2 (16-oz.) cans refried beans
1 (4-oz.) can whole California green chiles, rinsed,
    seeded, chopped
1 1/2 cups (6 oz.) shredded Monterey Jack cheese
1 1/2 cups (6 oz.) shredded sharp cheddar cheese
2 cups mild red taco sauce
1/2 cup chopped green onions
3/4 cup sliced pitted ripe olives
2 cups guacamole
1 cup sour cream

Heat large skillet over medium-high heat. Crumble beef and sausage into pan. Add onion; cook, stirring frequently, about 5 minutes or until meat is lightly browned and tender. Remove and discard fat. Season with hot pepper sauce and salt. Set aside to cool.

In 3-quart casserole, spread refried beans to cover bottom. Spread cooked meat evenly over beans. Sprinkle chiles over meat. Sprinkle cheeses over chiles. Drizzle red taco sauce over casserole.

Refrigerate, covered, up to 24 hours. Return to room temperature before baking.

Heat oven to 350°F. Bake casserole 20 to 30 minutes or until hot and bubbly. Remove casserole from oven; sprinkle green onions and olives on top. Mound guacamole in center; top with sour cream. Serve with tortilla chips, if desired.

CURTIS' CRAB DIP
SARAH (CURTIS) STRANGE

Curtis, the boys and I love to catch our own crabs off the dock at our house in Virginia Beach. Those we don't eat right away I use for this dip.

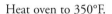

1 (1-lb.) pkg. crabmeat (jumbo or
    lump)
1 (8-oz.) pkg. cream cheese,
    softened
3 tablespoons white wine
$1/2$ teaspoon horseradish
2 tablespoons minced onion
Dash hot pepper sauce
$1/8$ teaspoon Worcestershire sauce

Heat oven to 350°F.

In large bowl, combine crabmeat, cream cheese, wine, horseradish, onion, hot pepper sauce and Worcestershire sauce; stir until well combined.

Place mixture in $1^1/2$-quart casserole. Bake 15 minutes. Serve with crackers, if desired.

SMOKED OYSTER APPETIZER
KRIS (TREVOR) DODDS

We found this recipe through Ilse and Tommy Tolles while travelling on the Hogan Tour in 1992. Since then it has been one of Trevor's favorites.

2 (8-oz.) cans smoked oysters, drained
1 teaspoon seasoned salt
1 teaspoon garlic powder
1 teaspoon freshly ground pepper
5 dashes hot pepper sauce
$1/4$ cup chopped red onion
$1/4$ cup chopped fresh parsley
2 tablespoons fresh lemon juice

In large bowl, combine oysters, salt, garlic powder, pepper, hot pepper sauce, red onion, parsley and lemon juice; mix until well blended.

Serve with sliced apples, figs or fruits, if desired.

HOT HEARTS OF PALM DIP
MARNIE (JAY) WILLIAMSON

Jay and I always serve this the week of the Bayhill International when we are at home and have many drop-by visitors. It is always the first hors d'oeuvre to disappear.

1 (8-oz.) can hearts of palm, drained, chopped
1 cup (4 oz.) shredded mozzarella cheese
$3/4$ cup mayonnaise
1 cup sour cream
3 tablespoons minced green onions
$1/4$ teaspoon garlic

Heat oven to 350°F. Spray 2-quart casserole with nonstick cooking spray.

In large bowl, combine hearts, cheese, mayonnaise, sour cream, onions and garlic; mix well. Transfer mixture to casserole. Bake 20 minutes or until bubbly. Serve with bread or crackers, if desired.

SAUSAGE DIP
BOBBI (CRAIG) BOWDEN

This recipe was stolen from friends Craig and I met at the Nike Shreveport Open. People hover over the stove when this appetizer is made; it is a sure winner.

1 (1-lb.) pkg. spicy sausage
1 (8-oz.) pkg. cream cheese, softened
1 (8-oz.) can diced tomatoes
1 (4-oz.) can green chiles

In heavy skillet, cook sausage until no longer pink in center.

Stir in cream cheese, tomatoes and chiles. Transfer mixture to slow cooker.

Warm mixture 30 minutes before serving. Serve with tortilla chips, if desired.

SAUSAGE SOUFFLE

CATHY (MARK) WIEBE

This recipe is a family favorite for Christmas morning. We put it in the oven before we open presents and when we are done it usually is too.

12 slices bread, trimmed, cubed
2 cups (8 oz.) shredded sharp cheddar cheese
1 1/2 lb. little smokies sausages
1 1/2 lb. Jimmy Dean sausage
6 eggs
3 cups milk
1 teaspoon dry mustard
1 1/2 (10 3/4-oz.) cans cream of mushroom soup

Spray 3-quart casserole with nonstick cooking spray.

Arrange bread in bottom of casserole. Sprinkle cheese over bread; top with smokies. In large skillet, cook sausage until no longer pink in center. Add to casserole.

In small bowl, beat eggs, 2 1/4 cups of the milk and dry mustard at high speed; pour over casserole. Refrigerate overnight.

Heat oven to 300°F. In large bowl, combine soup and remaining 3/4 cup milk; mix well. Spread mixture over casserole. Bake 1 1/2 to 2 hours or until set.

SALMON SPREAD

DENA (JOHN) MAGINNES

1 (14.75-oz.) can salmon
1 (8-oz.) pkg. cream cheese, softened
1 teaspoon horseradish
1/2 teaspoon salt
3 tablespoons chopped fresh parsley
1 tablespoon fresh lemon juice
2 tablespoons grated onion
1/2 teaspoon liquid smoke
1/2 cup chopped pecans or walnuts

Drain and discard bones from salmon.

In large bowl, combine cream cheese, horseradish, salt, 2 tablespoons of the parsley, lemon juice, onion, liquid smoke and 1/4 cup of the pecans; mix well. Refrigerate, covered, overnight.

Shape mixture into ball. In small bowl, combine remaining 1 tablespoon parsley and remaining 1/4 cup pecans. Roll ball in parsley mixture until evenly covered. Serve with crackers, if desired.

Salmon Spread

MEXICAN DIP

KRIS (TREVOR) DODDS

Although this recipe isn't extravagant, it is quick and easy to make, not to mention tasty.

1 (8-oz.) pkg. cream cheese, softened
1 (15-oz.) can chili without beans
1 (4-oz.) can green chiles, chopped
    Green onions, chopped (optional)
2 cups (8 oz.) finely shredded cheddar cheese

Heat oven to 350°F.

Spread cream cheese over bottom of 9-inch pie pan. Layer chili, chiles, green onions and cheddar cheese, in order, over cream cheese. Bake 20 minutes. Serve with tortilla chips, if desired.

FLINTSTONE BREAD DIP

TERRI (RICK) FEHR

1 cup sour cream
1 cup mayonnaise
1 tablespoon dried minced onion
$1/4$ teaspoon Beau Monde seasoning
1 pkg. chipped beef, coarsely chopped
Salt to taste
1 Flintstone (round) loaf bread

In large bowl, combine sour cream, mayonnaise, onion, Beau monde seasoning, beef and salt; mix well. Refrigerate, covered, several hours or overnight.

Cut domed top off bread. Hollow out bread by cutting 1 inch inside crust vertically all the way around and within 1 inch of bottom. Remove insides in one piece. Place bread bowl on serving platter. Cut leftover top and insides into 1-inch cubes; arrange cubes around bread bowl on platter.

Pour chilled dip into bread bowl and serve. After all pre-cut bread cubes are gone, have guests cut out and dip their own cubes from bread bowl.

LAYERED MEXICAN BEAN DIP

LAURA (JOHN) FLANNERY

1 (16-oz.) can vegetarian refried beans
1 cup sour cream
1 cup *Guacamole* (page 10)
1 tomato, chopped
1 (6-oz.) can ripe olives, drained
1 cup salsa
1 cup (4 oz.) finely shredded cheddar cheese

In bottom of 2-quart casserole, spread layer of refried beans. Top in layers with half of sour cream, guacamole, tomatoes, black olives and salsa. Sprinkle with layer of cheese. Repeat layers. Top with cheese. Serve with tortilla chips, if desired.

ARIZONA GUACAMOLE

SANDRA (RONNIE) BLACK

Ronnie and I serve this at our Tucson Open Dinner and all our guests make birdies, birdies, birdies.

6 large Haas avocados
1 pint cottage cheese
1 tablespoon fresh lemon juice
2 jalapeño chiles, chopped, juice reserved
$1/4$ teaspoon salt
$1/4$ teaspoon freshly ground pepper
$1/4$ teaspoon garlic salt
$1/4$ teaspoon lemon-pepper seasoning

In medium bowl, combine avocado and cottage cheese; mash until smooth. Stir in lemon juice and chiles. Add jalapeño juice, salt, pepper, garlic salt and lemon pepper; mix well. Serve with corn chips or over enchiladas, if desired. Store in refrigerator.

CHEDDAR DIP

JUDI (WAYNE) LEVI

This is a favorite with Wayne and I because it is delicious, yet so easy to make.

1 cup finely chopped onion
1 cup mayonnaise
1 cup (4 oz.) shredded cheddar cheese

Heat oven to 300°F. Spray 2-quart casserole with nonstick cooking spray.

In medium bowl, combine onion, mayonnaise and cheese; mix until well blended. Spread mixture in casserole. Bake 15 minutes or until browned.

CHEESE AND TUNA HORS D'OEUVRES

SHARON (DAVID) OGRIN

This recipe is a favorite of David's. It is popular at our house because the rolls freeze well and can be taken out when a quick snack is needed.

1 loaf white bread, frozen
$1^1/2$ cups butter, melted
1 (1-lb.) loaf processed cheese spread, cubed
2 (6-oz.) cans tuna, drained, mashed

Heat oven to 350°. Spray 13x9-inch pan with nonstick cooking spray.

Remove crusts from bread and slice remaining loaf. Roll slices flat with rolling pan.

In heavy skillet, heat $^1/2$ cup of the butter and cheese over medium heat until melted; add tuna.

Spread mixture over bread slices; roll up. Cut rolls in half; dip rolls in remaining 1 cup butter. Place rolls in pan. Bake 20 minutes.

BROCCOLI DIP IN FRENCH BREAD

CATHI (KIRK) TRIPLETT

1 round loaf French bread
1 (10-oz.) pkg. frozen chopped broccoli, thawed, drained
1 cup sour cream
1 cup mayonnaise
2 tablespoons diced green onion
2 tablespoons chopped fresh parsley
1 (2-oz.) jar chopped pimiento, drained
$^1/2$ teaspoon dill weed
$^1/4$ teaspoon salt
$^1/8$ teaspoon minced garlic

Cut $1^1/2$-inch slice off top of loaf; set aside. Hollow out bottom leaving thick shell. Cut or tear slice from top of loaf and bread from inside into bite-size pieces.

In large bowl, combine broccoli, sour cream, mayonnaise, onion, parsley, pimiento, dill weed, salt and garlic; mix well. Pour mixture into bread bowl. Garnish with torn bread from center and vegetables.

SALSA

DIANNE (TED) SCHULZ

2 (14.5-oz.) cans diced tomatoes
2 garlic cloves, minced
$^1/2$ red onion, chopped
$^1/2$ green bell pepper, chopped
1 teaspoon dried oregano
1 tablespoon fresh lime juice
1 (12-oz.) jar hot salsa
$^1/2$ bunch cilantro, chopped
$^1/8$ teaspoon salt
$^1/8$ teaspoon freshly ground pepper

In food processor, combine tomatoes, garlic, onion, bell pepper, oregano, lime juice, salsa, cilantro, salt and pepper; chop 10 to 20 seconds. Refrigerate 24 hours before serving.

CHINESE TACOS

CATHI (KIRK) TRIPLETT

This recipe is one of my favorites. Its uniqueness is bound to bring plenty of compliments to the cook.

1 lb. cooked pork, chicken or beef, minced
1/2 cup minced celery
1/4 cup minced onion
2 tablespoons minced mushrooms
Dash ground white pepper
1 tablespoon soy sauce
3/4 teaspoon curry powder
3/4 lb. wonton wrappers
1/4 cup vegetable oil

In large bowl, combine meat, celery, onion, mushrooms, pepper, soy sauce and curry powder; mix well. Place 1 teaspoon of mixture on center of each wonton. Wet edges of wrapper with water; fold over filling, forming rectangle. Pleat open edges; press to seal.

In large skillet, heat oil over medium-high heat until temperature reaches 375°F. Cook wontons until golden brown. Drain on paper towels.

MAROON CLOUD CHEESE DIP

TRACY (BRIAN) CLAAR

Don't be led astray by the simple ingredients; this recipe is surprisingly good! Brian and I always serve this at our get-togethers.

6 cups (1 1/2 lb.) finely shredded white cheddar cheese
1/4 cup chopped white onion
1/3 cup mayonnaise
Raspberry preserves

Heat oven to 350°F. Spray 3-quart casserole with nonstick cooking spray.

In casserole, combine cheese, onion and mayonnaise; mix well. Bake until cheese is melted and browned. Top with raspberry preserves. Serve with crackers.

CAJUN CHICKEN THUMB BITS

SUZANNE (DUDLEY) HART

This dish is one of Dudley's favorite appetizers.

4 tablespoons olive oil
2 tablespoons chopped fresh basil
1 bunch fresh parsley
1/2 loaf French bread, sliced 1/4 inch thick (about 24 slices)
4 boneless skinless chicken breast halves, cubed
1 1/2 teaspooons Cajun seasoning
1 garlic clove, minced
3 plum tomatoes, sliced
3 dill pickles, sliced

Heat oven to 350°F.

In medium bowl, combine 3 tablespoons of the olive oil, basil and parsley; mix well. Lightly spread mixture over bread slices. Arrange bread slices on ungreased baking sheet. Bake 8 minutes or until light golden brown.

In large skillet, heat remaining 1 tablespoon oil over medium-high heat until hot. Add chicken; sprinkle with Cajun seasoning. Cook chicken until no longer pink in center. Remove from heat.

On serving platter, place garlic to taste on each toasted bread slice; add chicken. Top with tomato and pickle slices.

 2

SOUPS & SALADS

ORIENTAL CHICKEN SALAD

DIANE (KEVIN) WENTWORTH

This is one of Kevin's absolute favorites! It is great for lunch or for a snack after practicing out on the golf course.

3 boneless skinless chicken breast halves
1 head green cabbage, chopped
1 bunch green onions, sliced
1 (8-oz.) can water chestnuts, drained, diced
4 packages dry ramen noodles
$1/2$ cup slivered almonds, if desired
$1/2$ cup sliced carrots, if desired
$1/2$ cup vegetable oil
2 to 4 tablespoons sugar
6 tablespoons red wine vinegar
1 tablespoon dark sesame oil

In large pot, cover chicken with water; heat over medium-high heat until boiling. Cook until chicken juices run clear; set aside. Cut chicken into bite-size pieces. In large bowl, combine chicken, cabbage, onions and water chestnuts; mix well.

With palm of your hand, crush each package of ramen noodles. Open packages, adding noodles to large bowl. Set aside seasoning mix. Add almonds and carrots.

In small bowl, stir together oil, sugar, red wine vinegar, sesame oil and 4 packages ramen seasoning. Add to large bowl; mix until well blended. Refrigerate up to 2 hours before serving.

EASY BRUNSWICK STEW

RYNDEE (MICHAEL) CLARK

The recipe originally came from Mike's mom. Mike and I really enjoy its classic Southern taste.

1 (32-oz.) can Brunswick stew
1 (16-oz.) can barbecue beef
1 (16-oz.) can barbecue pork
2 (16-oz.) cans stewed tomatoes
1 (14.75-oz.) can whole kernel corn
1 cup cubed cooked chicken breast

In large stockpot, combine stew, beef, pork, tomatoes, corn and chicken. Simmer over medium heat 4 hours, stirring occasionally.

HAMBURGER SOUP

SUE (JOEY) SINDELAR

5 cups water
2 lb. ground beef, cooked
1 Spanish onion, chopped
1 (14.5-oz.) can whole tomatoes
$1/2$ cup chopped celery
3 potatoes, cubed
$1/2$ cup chopped carrots
$1/2$ cup frozen peas, thawed
$1/2$ cup frozen corn, thawed
$1/4$ teaspoon salt
$1/4$ teaspoon freshly ground pepper

In large pot, combine water, beef, onion, tomatoes, celery, potatoes, carrots, peas, corn, salt and pepper. Simmer over low heat in slow cooker 6 to 8 hours, stirring occasionally. Serve hot with warm bread, if desired.

BLACK BEAN SOUP

CYNDI (JIM) CARTER

2 tablespoons vegetable oil
1 medium onion, chopped
2 garlic cloves, minced
1 teaspoon dried oregano
1 teaspoon ground cumin
1 (14.5-oz.) can diced tomatoes
$1/4$ cup salsa
2 (15-oz.) cans black beans, drained, not rinsed
1 (14.5-oz.) can reduced-sodium chicken broth

In large saucepan, heat oil over medium-high heat until hot. Add onion, garlic, oregano and cumin; cook, stirring constantly, 3 to 5 minutes or until onions are browned. Add tomatoes, salsa, black beans and chicken broth. Bring to a boil and cook 5 minutes, stirring frequently.

If desired, puree soup in blender or food processor. Return soup to saucepan and cook over medium to low heat 5 to 7 minutes, stirring frequently, until hot.

BLACK BEAN SOUP

ITALIAN DRESSING

TILLIE BABIN (STEWART CINK'S GRANDMOTHER)

This recipe is excellent for salads of all kinds. You may also use this dressing to marinate shrimp, avocado, tomato and artichokes.

1 1/2 cups vegetable oil
1/2 cup vinegar
1/4 cup sugar
1/2 cup ketchup
3/4 teaspoon salt
1 garlic clove, minced
1/8 teaspoon paprika

In jar with tight-fitting lid, combine oil, vinegar, sugar, ketchup, salt, garlic and paprika; cover and shake well. Refrigerate up to 12 hours before serving.

APPLE-SPINACH SALAD

LAUREN (JIM) MCGOVERN

Jimmy absolutely hates every kind of spinach except this salad! This recipe is from my mother and is always one of the first dishes to disappear at our parties.

1 (10-oz.) pkg. fresh
    spinach, torn
2 Granny Smith
    apples, chopped
1/2 cup cashews
1/2 cup golden raisins
1/4 cup sugar
1/4 cup apple cider
    vinegar
1/4 cup vegetable oil
1/4 teaspoon garlic salt
1/4 teaspoon celery salt

In medium bowl, combine spinach, apples, cashews and raisins; mix well.

In jar, combine sugar, vinegar, oil, garlic salt and celery salt; cover tightly. Shake vigorously. Refrigerate before serving. Pour dressing over salad; toss to coat.

9-LAYER SALAD

SHIRLEY (BILLY) CASPER

This recipe originates from my fond memories of living in Mapleton, Utah, a little farm town nestled in the Wasatch Mountains. Billy and I enjoy the lovely look and taste of this salad.

1 1/2 cups finely shredded lettuce
1/2 cup finely chopped green onion
1/2 cup finely chopped celery
1/2 cup finely chopped cucumbers
1/2 cup finely chopped water chestnuts
1/2 cup finely chopped carrots
1/2 cup finely chopped broccoli florets
1/2 cup frozen peas, thawed
1/2 cup crumbled cooked bacon, well-drained
2 cups mayonnaise
1/2 to 1 cup (2 to 4 oz.) freshly grated Parmesan
    cheese
1/4 teaspoon garlic salt
1/4 teaspoon onion salt
1/4 teaspoon freshly ground pepper
1/4 teaspoon fresh dill
2 tablespoons oil
3 tablespoons vinegar

In 3-quart casserole, sprinkle lettuce over bottom followed by onion, celery, cucumbers, water chestnuts, carrots, broccoli, peas and bacon.

In small bowl, combine mayonnaise, cheese, garlic salt, onion salt, pepper, dill, oil and vinegar; mix until well blended. Spread dressing over top layer of salad. Refrigerate, covered, at least 15 hours. Garnish with sliced, hard-boiled eggs, tomatoes, red, green and yellow bell peppers and sunflower seeds, if desired.

MEXICAN BLACK BEAN AND CORN SALAD

CATHY (BRIAN) HENNINGER

2 ears corn
4 cups cooked black beans, or 3 (15-oz.) cans black
   beans, drained
2 cups cooked rice
$^1/_2$ cup chopped red bell pepper
$^1/_2$ small red onion, chopped
$^1/_2$ cup tarragon vinegar
$^1/_3$ cup vegetable oil
$^3/_4$ teaspoon ground cumin
$^3/_4$ teaspoon chili powder
1 garlic clove, minced
1 teaspoon honey

In medium saucepan, steam corn until tender but still crisp. Cut corn kernals from cobs. In large bowl, combine beans, corn, rice, bell pepper and onion; mix well.

In small bowl, combine vinegar, oil, cumin, chili powder, garlic and honey; stir until well blended. Pour dressing over salad mixture; toss well. Refrigerate 1 hour before serving.

FRENCH DRESSING

DENA (JOHN) MAGINNES

2 cups salad oil
2 tablespoons packed brown sugar
$^1/_2$ cup white vinegar
3 tablespoons ketchup
1 teaspoon salt
1 teaspoon paprika
$^1/_8$ teaspoon grated onion
$^1/_2$ egg white, unbeaten
1 garlic clove, minced

In large bowl, whisk together oil, brown sugar, vinegar, ketchup, salt, paprika, onion, egg white and garlic. Refrigerate 1 hour before serving.

Mexican Black Bean and Corn Salad

LETTUCE-PEA SALAD

CATHI (KIRK) TRIPLETT

This recipe, originally from Kirk's mother, is perfect for family gatherings and picnics. This salad will surely bring the compliments, from its presentation to its taste.

1 cup frozen peas, thawed
3 cups torn lettuce
1 cup diced celery
1/2 cup chopped onion
1 cup mayonnaise
2 tablespoons sugar
1/2 cup (2 oz.) shredded cheddar cheese
1/2 cup cooked bacon, crumbled

In large bowl, combine peas, lettuce, celery and onion; set aside. In another bowl, combine mayonnaise and sugar; mix until well combined. Combine greens and mayonnaise mixture.

Sprinkle cheese and bacon over greens; cover. Refrigerate at least 4 hours or overnight.

SHRIMP SALAD

DENA (JOHN) MAGINNES

This recipe works great for parties, showers, picnics or any occasion.

2 lb. shelled, deveined cooked large shrimp
1/2 cup *French Dressing* (page 25)
1 1/2 tablespoons finely grated onion
1/2 cup finely grated green bell pepper
1/2 cup finely grated celery
1 teaspoon salt
1/2 teaspoon freshly ground pepper
1 teaspoon hot pepper sauce
1 teaspoon Worcestershire sauce
1 cup mayonnaise
2 hard-cooked eggs, chopped

In large bowl, combine shrimp, French Dressing, onion, green bell pepper, celery, salt, pepper, hot pepper sauce and Worcestershire sauce; mix well. Cover and refrigerate 30 minutes. Fold in mayonnaise and eggs. Serve chilled.

JARLSBERG VEGETABLE BISQUE

SUE (JOEY) SINDELAR

3 tablespoons butter
3 tablespoons all-purpose flour
4 cups chicken stock or 2 (14.5-oz.) cans reduced-sodium chicken broth
2 cups coarsely chopped broccoli
3/4 cup chopped carrots
1/2 cup chopped celery
1 small onion, chopped
1 small garlic clove, minced
1/4 teaspoon thyme, crushed
1/2 teaspoon salt
1/8 teaspoon freshly ground pepper
1 cup heavy cream
1 egg yolk
1 1/2 cups (6 oz.) shredded Jarlsberg cheese

In large saucepan, heat butter over medium-high heat until melted. Add flour; cook several minutes, stirring constantly. Remove from heat. Gradually blend in broth. Bring to a boil, stirring occasionally. Add vegetables and seasonings; simmer, covered, 8 minutes or until vegetables are tender.

In small bowl, blend cream and egg yolk. Gradually blend in several tablespoons of soup. Return cream mixture to saucepan and continue to cook 5 minutes. Stir in cheese until blended. Serve warm.

RED POTATO SALAD

LINDA (BOBBY) WADKINS

1 1/2 lb. new red potatoes, quartered (1 inch thick)
2 ribs celery, diced
3/4 cup bottled ranch dressing
4 spring onions, diced
1 teaspoon salt
1 teaspoon freshly ground pepper

In large saucepan, boil potatoes 15 to 20 minutes or until tender. Remove potatoes from water; rinse and dry.

In large bowl, combine potatoes, celery, dressing, onion sprigs, salt and pepper; toss until well combined. Refrigerate salad overnight.

Red Potato Salad

BEAN SOUP

KATHY (ROBERT) WRENN

Robert and I love to make the dry bean mixture for this soup, place it in a mason jar with the recipe attached and give it to friends as gifts. This soup is wonderful with corn bread.

2 cups 16-bean mixture
2 teaspoons salt
1 lb. ham, diced
1 to 2 garlic cloves, minced
1 large onion, diced
1/4 cup fresh lemon juice
1 (10-oz.) can ro-tel tomatoes
1 (14.5-oz.) can tomatoes
1/2 to 1 lb. sliced Polish sausage

Rinse beans. Cover with water, add 1 teaspoon salt and soak overnight. (Or bring beans to a boil 5 minutes, remove from heat and soak 1 hour). Drain. Place beans in 2 quarts water with 1/2 to 1 teaspoon salt; add ham and bring to a boil. Add garlic and onion.

Simmer, covered, 2 to 3 hours or until beans are tender. Add lemon juice and tomatoes; simmer 1 hour. Add sausage; simmer an additional 30 minutes.

GOURMET MUSHROOM SOUP

KRIS (TREVOR) DODDS

Trevor enjoys soup any time of the year, and as far as he is concerned, it does not have to be cold outside. Though I think it tastes better fireside.

2 tablespoons olive oil

1 tablespoon butter

1 onion, chopped

2 leeks, chopped

1 sprig fresh rosemary

1 (6-oz.) can brown mushrooms, thinly sliced

3 tablespoons plus 1 teaspoon all-purpose flour

3 cups chicken broth or 1 1/2 (14.5-oz.) cans reduced-sodium chicken broth

1/4 teaspoon salt

1/4 teaspoon freshly ground pepper

Dash ground mace

1 cup milk

1 teaspoon soy sauce

Pinch sugar

2 tablespoons sherry

3 tablespoons plus 1 teaspoon heavy cream

In Dutch oven, heat oil and butter over medium-high heat until hot. Sauté onion and leeks until tender. Add rosemary and one-half of the mushrooms to mixture; fry until tender. Remove rosemary; stir in flour.

Slowly add broth, stirring constantly. Season broth with salt, pepper and mace. Simmer, covered, 15 minutes. Set aside; cool 10 minutes.

Pour mixture into food processor; puree until smooth. Return mixture to Dutch oven; add remaining mushrooms, milk, soy sauce and sugar. Cover and simmer 10 minutes. Add sherry; swirl in cream. Serve immediately garnished with fried onion rings, if desired.

TORTILLA SOUP

DIANNE (TED) SCHULZ

Ted and I love this soup chunky! It is so hearty and filling, especially on a brisk fall day or just after a long day at the golf course.

6 cups chicken broth or 3 1/2 (14.5-oz.) cans reduced-sodium chicken broth

2 tablespoons fresh lime juice

3 teaspoons cumin

5 teaspoons chili powder

1/2 teaspoon salt

1/2 teaspoon freshly ground pepper

6 carrots, sliced

5 ribs celery, sliced

3 large onions, sliced

1/2 bunch cilantro

1 lb. frozen corn

1 (14.5-oz.) can diced tomatoes

Bring broth to a boil over medium-high heat; add lime juice, cumin, chili powder, salt and pepper, stirring occasionally. Add carrots, celery, onions, cilantro, corn and tomatoes. Cook until vegetables are just tender.

Simmer, uncovered, 2 1/2 hours. Serve with crushed tortilla chips and shredded cheese, if desired.

CAESAR SALAD DRESSING

JAN (PETER) JACOBSEN

Peter got this recipe from his mother. He likes it so much he personally called her up and wrote down the recipe to add to my files.

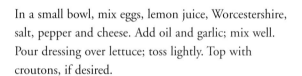

4 eggs, beaten
$1/2$ cup fresh lemon juice
1 teaspoon Worcestershire sauce
$1/8$ teaspoon salt
$1/8$ teaspoon freshly ground
    pepper, plus more to taste
1 cup (4 oz.) freshly grated
    Parmesan cheese
3 garlic cloves, crushed
1 head Romaine lettuce
1 cup oil

In a small bowl, mix eggs, lemon juice, Worcestershire, salt, pepper and cheese. Add oil and garlic; mix well. Pour dressing over lettuce; toss lightly. Top with croutons, if desired.

BROCCOLI SALAD

BONNIE (LARRY) MIZE

This recipe was first enjoyed when my sister Mary had all of our sisters and families over for a meal. Larry and I loved it and couldn't quit eating it.

2 heads broccoli, chopped into bite-size pieces
1 cup chopped red onion
1 cup raisins
1 cup mayonnaise
$1/2$ cup sugar
3 tablespoons vinegar
8 thick slices bacon, cooked, crumbled

In large bowl, combine broccoli, onion and raisins; mix well. Set aside.

In jar, combine mayonnaise, sugar and vinegar; cover and shake vigorously. Pour over broccoli mixture to coat; toss. Top with crumbled bacon.

HOT AND SOUR SHRIMP SOUP

KULTIDA WOODS (TIGER'S MOM)

2 stalks lemon grass
2 kaffir lime leaves
1 cup sliced fresh mushrooms
$1/2$ teaspoon salt
10 shelled, deveined uncooked medium shrimp
2 tablespoons nampla (fish sauce)
2 tablespoons lemon or lime juice
$1/2$ teaspoon chili powder
Fresh coriander

Fill medium saucepan half full of water; heat to a boil. Add lemon grass, lime leaves, mushrooms and salt.

Drop in shrimp; simmer gently 3 minutes or until shrimp turn pink. Remove from heat; season with nampla, lemon juice and chili powder. Spoon into individual bowls. Garnish with sprigs of fresh coriander. Serve hot.

FRUIT SALAD

CISSYE (JIM) GALLAGHER

Jim would not think of eating any other fruit salad! This recipe is just the touch you need to top off a duck dinner (page 70)— perfect for a meat and potatoes eater.

1 cup mayonnaise
2 teaspoons fresh lemon juice
$1/4$ cup sugar
2 apples, chopped
2 bananas, sliced
1 bunch grapes, sliced

In medium bowl, combine mayonnaise, lemon juice and sugar; mix until well blended and smooth. Pour over fruit. Refrigerate at least 2 hours before serving.

BLUEBERRY GELATIN SALAD

CHRISTY (TOM) KITE

This recipe was first introduced to me at the Byron Nelson Golf Classic. It was served by Byron and Louise Nelson and has since become one of Tom's favorites.

1 (^{1}/4-oz.) pkg. red raspberry gelatin
1 (^{1}/4-oz.) pkg. black raspberry gelatin
1 (8-oz.) pkg. cream cheese, softened
1 (4-oz.) can blueberries, drained, liquid reserved
1 cup chopped nuts

Measure drained blueberry juice. Add juice and 3^1/2 cups boiling water to large pot. In food processor mix cream cheese with reserved ^{1}/4 cup juice. Dissolve jello in remaining 3^3/4 cups. Add fruit, nuts and cheese mixture; pour into gelatin mold. Refrigerate until set.

CHICKEN VEGETABLE NOODLE SOUP

CYNTHIA (MARK) BROOKS

This is a favorite recipe from "Mrs. Burdick's Cookbook" that is often enjoyed by our family.

^{1}/2 fryer chicken, boiled, cut into bite-size pieces
^{1}/2 cup sliced carrots
1 cup sliced celery
3 teaspoons chicken bouillon
^{1}/4 cup minced onion
1 tablespoon margarine
^{1}/2 teaspoon salt
^{1}/2 teaspoon freshly ground pepper
1^1/2 cups thin egg noodles

Measure broth from boiled chicken; add water to make 6 cups.

In large pot, combine broth, water, carrots, celery, bouillon, onion, margarine, salt and pepper; stir. Add noodles; boil 5 to 10 minutes or until noodles are cooked.

CHINESE CABBAGE SALAD

BARBARA (JACK) NICKLAUS

SALAD
1 head cabbage
4 green onions, chopped
1 to 2 (3-oz.) pkg. ramen noodles
1 (2-oz.) pkg. almonds, sliced or slivered
^{1}/4 cup sesame seeds

DRESSING
^{1}/2 cup sugar
^{1}/4 cup vinegar
^{3}/4 cup oil
2 tablespoons soy sauce

To prepare salad, slice cabbage crosswise. In large bowl, combine cabbage and onions. Break up ramen noodles; sprinkle over cabbage and onions. Add almonds and sesame seeds.

For dressing, in small pot, boil sugar, vinegar, oil and soy sauce. Cool. Pour over salad; toss.

SPAGHETTI SALAD

JODIE MUDD

I make this dish often because it is delicious and so quick and easy.

1 (16-oz.) pkg. vermicelli spaghetti
1 green bell pepper, chopped
1 onion, chopped
1 cucumber, peeled, sliced
3 ribs celery, chopped
2 to 3 tomatoes, diced
Salad Supreme Seasoning to taste
Zesty Italian Dressing to taste

Cook spaghetti according to package directions; drain. In large bowl, combine cooked spaghetti, bell pepper, onion, cucumber, celery and tomatoes. Add seasoning and dressing. Serve chilled.

CHINESE CHICKEN SALAD

ANNE CINK (STEWART'S MOM)

SALAD

1 cup cooked chicken, cut into 1-inch strips
1 head cabbage, chopped
1 bunch green onions
1 tablespoon butter
$^1/_2$ cup sesame seeds
1 (2-oz.) pkg. sliced almonds
2 (3-oz.) pkg. ramen noodles

DRESSING

6 tablespoons rice vinegar
4 tablespoons sugar
1 cup olive oil
1 teaspoon Accent
2 chicken-flavor packets from ramen noodles
$^1/_8$ teaspoon freshly ground pepper plus more to taste

To prepare salad, in large bowl, combine chicken, cabbage and onions. In large skillet, sauté butter, sesame seeds, almonds and uncooked noodles 2 minutes. Add to cabbage mixture.

For dressing, in small bowl, combine vinegar, sugar, oil, Accent, flavoring packets and pepper; mix well. Add to salad just before serving; toss well.

NEW ENGLAND CLAM CHOWDER

JAN (JAY) HAAS

12 thick slices bacon, cooked, crumbled
$^1/_2$ cup minced onion
2 (10$^3/_4$-oz.) cans cream of potato soup
2 cups half-and-half
2 (10-oz.) cans minced clams, undrained
2 tablespoons fresh lemon juice
$^1/_4$ teaspoon freshly ground pepper

In medium saucepan, combine bacon, onion, soup, half-and-half, clams, lemon juice and pepper; cook over medium heat until hot, stiring constantly.

HOLIDAY CRANBERRY SALAD

ANNE CINK (STEWART'S MOM)

This dish is super quick and easy. As the name states, it works perfect for any holiday celebration meal.

1 cup sugar
$^1/_2$ cup cranberry juice
$^1/_8$ teaspoon salt
1 pkg. fresh cranberries

In large bowl, combine sugar, cranberry juice and salt; mix well. Add cranberries. Microwave on High 10 minutes; do not stir. Rinse bowl with very cold water to chill. Pour cooked sauce into bowl. Refrigerate 3 to 4 hours or until set.

MANDARIN TOSS SALAD

JAN (JAY) HAAS

SALAD

1 head Romaine lettuce
1 head Bibb lettuce
4 green onions with tops, sliced
2 (11-oz.) cans mandarin oranges, drained
1 cup chopped pecans, toasted
1 avocado, peeled, sliced
Freshly ground pepper to taste

DRESSING

1/2 cup oil
4 tablespoons sugar
2 tablespoons parsley, chopped
1 teaspoon salt
Dash freshly ground pepper

To prepare salad, tear lettuce into bite-size pieces and place in salad bowl. Add green onions and orange segments. Just before serving, add pecans and avocado; grind fresh pepper over salad.

To prepare dressing, in small jar, combine oil, sugar, vinegar, parsley, salt and pepper. Cover and shake vigorously. Refrigerate.

Pour dressing over salad. Toss and serve immediately.

PENNSYLVANIA CHICKEN NOODLE SOUP

JENNIFER (GLEN) RALSTON-DAY

Glen and I like to add a pinch of saffron to this broth for an authentic flavor of the Pennsylvania Dutch.

2 tablespoons butter
1 rib celery, finely chopped
1 carrot, finely chopped
1/2 cup finely chopped onion
1 (1 1/2-lb.) boneless skinless
    chicken breast
1 quart chicken stock
1/8 teaspoon saffron threads
1 (6-oz.) pkg. noodles, narrow, wide or Dutch
1 cup corn, frozen (thawed) or canned
1/4 teaspoon freshly ground pepper

In large saucepan, heat butter over medium-high heat until melted. Stir in celery, carrot and onion. Coat with butter; add chicken. Cook, covered, over medium-high heat, turning several times, 10 to 15 minutes or until chicken juices are clear.

Remove chicken. Cut into small cubes; set aside. Add chicken broth and saffron to saucepan. Bring to a rapid boil. Add noodles and corn. Simmer, covered, 15 minutes or until noodles are just done.

Remove 2 cups of soup, place in blender and blend until smooth. Return mixture to soup. Add chicken. Heat 1 to 2 minutes or until hot. Season with pepper.

BREADS & MUFFINS

JANE'S BANANA BREAD

JODY (BILLY) ANDRADE

During the week of the Kemper Open in 1991, Billy was first introduced to this banana bread. He had it every morning for breakfast and it worked like magic on his appetite and his game.

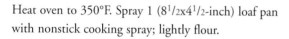

1/2 cup vegetable oil
1 cup sugar
2 eggs, beaten
3 to 4 cups mashed
    bananas (about 6)
2 cups all-purpose flour
1 teaspoon baking
    soda
1/2 teaspoon baking powder
1/2 teaspoon salt
3 tablespoons milk
1/2 teaspoon vanilla
1 cup chopped walnuts

Heat oven to 350°F. Spray 1 (8^1/2x4^1/2-inch) loaf pan with nonstick cooking spray; lightly flour.

In large bowl, beat oil and sugar at medium speed. Add eggs and bananas; continue beating at medium speed until well combined.

In another large bowl, combine flour, baking soda, baking powder and salt; stir into egg mixture and mix well. Add milk and vanilla; mix thoroughly. Stir in nuts; pour batter into pan. Bake 1 hour or until toothpick inserted near center comes out clean.

ZUCCHINI BREAD

WINNIE (ARNOLD) PALMER

4 eggs
1^1/2 cups sugar
1 cup vegetable oil
3^1/2 cups all-purpose flour
1^1/2 teaspoons baking soda
1^1/2 teaspoons salt
1 teaspoon cinnamon
3/4 teaspoon baking powder
2 cups grated zucchini
1 teaspoon vanilla
1 cup chopped nuts
1 cup raisins, if desired

Heat oven to 350°F. Spray 2 (8^1/2x4^1/2-inch) loaf pans with nonstick cooking spray.

In large bowl, beat eggs, sugar and oil at medium speed until thoroughly blended.

In another large bowl, combine flour, baking soda, salt, cinnamon and baking powder; add to egg mixture. Stir in zucchini, vanilla, nuts and raisins. Pour batter into pans, filling half full. Bake 45 to 55 minutes or until browned.

HEALTHY BANANA-NUT BREAD

LAURA (JOHN) FLANNERY

$^1/_2$ cup margarine
1 cup packed brown sugar
2 eggs, beaten
3 bananas, mashed
2 cups whole wheat flour
1 teaspoon baking soda
1 teaspoon salt
2 cups chopped nuts

Heat oven to 350°F. Spray 8-inch square pan with nonstick cooking spray.

In large bowl, beat margarine and brown sugar at medium speed until light and fluffy. Beat in eggs; add bananas to mixture. In medium bowl, combine flour, baking soda and salt; add to egg mixture. Stir well. Stir in nuts until well blended.

Pour batter into pan. Bake 1 hour.

BEER-CHEESE BREAD

AMY (CHRIS) DIMARCO
We have found this bread to be a huge success at parties. You can make it low-fat by using fat-free or low-fat cheese and it is just as tasty.

2 (8-oz.) pkg. cream cheese, softened
1 (1-lb.) loaf processed cheese spread, cubed
$^1/_2$ cup beer
1 teaspoon garlic powder
1 loaf French bread

In medium saucepan, heat cream cheese, cheese, beer and garlic powder over medium-high heat until smooth and creamy. Set aside.

Make a "bowl" in bread by removing middle of loaf in small pieces. Fill "bowl" with cheese mixture; place torn pieces of bread over top. Serve immediately.

POPPY SEED BREAD

SUE (JOEY) SINDELAR

BREAD
3 eggs
$1^1/_2$ cups milk
$1^1/_2$ cups vegetable oil
$1^1/_2$ teaspoons almond extract
$1^1/_2$ teaspoons butter
$1^1/_2$ teaspoons vanilla
$2^1/_4$ cups sugar
3 cups all-purpose flour
$1^1/_2$ teaspoons salt
$1^1/_2$ teaspoons baking powder
$1^1/_2$ tablespoons poppy seeds

GLAZE
$^1/_4$ cup orange juice
$^3/_4$ cup sugar
$^1/_2$ teaspoon almond extract
$^1/_2$ teaspoon butter
$^1/_2$ teaspoon vanilla

Heat oven to 325°F. Spray 2 ($8^1/_2$x$4^1/_2$-inch) loaf pans with nonstick cooking spray.

In large bowl, combine eggs, milk, oil, $1^1/_2$ teaspoons almond extract, $1^1/_2$ teaspoons butter flavoring and $1^1/_2$ teaspoons vanilla. Stir in $2^1/_4$ cups sugar, flour, salt, baking powder and poppy seeds. Pour into pans. Bake 1 hour or until toothpick inserted near center comes out clean. Cool on wire rack 10 minutes. Remove from pan; drizzle with glaze.

To prepare glaze, in large bowl, combine orange juice, $^3/_4$ cup sugar, $^1/_2$ teaspoon almond extract, $^1/_2$ teaspoon butter flavoring and $^1/_2$ teaspoon vanilla; mix until well blended. Drizzle over bread.

DI'S DELICIOUS FRENCH TOAST

DIANE (FRANK) LICKLITER

Since we travel nine months out of the year, Frank requests French toast when we are at home. Over the years, other Tour playing houseguests have gotten accustomed to Di's French toast too.

6 large eggs

2 tablespoons milk

1 tablespoon vanilla

1 teaspoon cinnamon

2 tablespoons butter, plus
    more for each slice of toast

12 slices Texas toast

In shallow, flat-bottomed bowl, whisk together eggs, milk, vanilla, and cinnamon.

Melt butter in large skillet over medium-high heat.

Dip both sides of bread into egg mixture; place bread in skillet. Cook until golden brown; turn and add dab of butter to cooked side. Serve with powdered sugar or syrup, if desired.

Di's Delicious French Toast

BAKING POWDER BISCUITS

CATHI (KIRK) TRIPLETT

3 cups all-purpose flour
1 1/2 tablespoons baking powder
3/4 teaspoon salt
8 tablespoons unsalted butter
1 cup milk

Heat oven to 450°F.

In large bowl, combine flour, baking powder and salt. Cut in butter; blend until mixture resembles fine crumbs. Add milk; stir with fork until soft dough is formed. Turn onto lightly floured board and knead 10 to 15 times.

Roll dough into 10-inch circle, about 1/2- to 3/4-inch thick. Cut out rounds with 2 1/2-inch plain biscuit cutter. Reform scraps, roll out and cut into rounds until dough is used up.

Place biscuits on ungreased baking sheet. Bake 12 to 14 minutes or until golden brown. Cool on paper towels.

BANANA BREAD

JAN (JAY) HAAS

1/2 cup oil
1 1/2 cups sugar
2 eggs
1 1/2 cups all-purpose flour
1 teaspoon baking soda
1/2 teaspoon salt
4 ripe bananas
4 tablespoons buttermilk
1 cup chopped pecans

Heat oven to 375°F. Spray 1 (8 1/2x4 1/2-inch) loaf pan with nonstick cooking spray; lightly flour.

In large bowl, cream oil and sugar. Add eggs; beat at high speed. Sift in flour, soda and salt.

In another large bowl, mash bananas. Combine bananas with creamed mixture. Add buttermilk and nuts; mix well.

Bake 45 minutes; let stand 15 minutes before slicing.

SPOON BREAD

CISSYE (JIM) GALLAGHER

Jim and I adore this truly southern tradition and it is even more wonderful with lemon/butter sauce poured over the top.

1 cup cornmeal
1 teaspoon salt
1 cup water
3 cups milk
3 eggs, beaten
1 teaspoon butter
1 teaspoon sugar

Heat oven to 375°F. Spray 1 1/2-quart casserole with nonstick cooking spray.

In medium saucepan, combine cornmeal and salt; stir in water.

Gradually add milk, stirring until smooth. Place over low heat; cook, stirring constantly, until thickened.

In medium bowl, spoon small amount of cornmeal mixture into eggs; mix well. Add egg mixture to saucepan, stirring constantly. Add butter and sugar; stir well. Pour mixture into casserole. Bake 40 to 50 minutes.

FRENCH BREAD

SOOZI (JERRY) PATE

This recipe is so flavorful and easy that it is sure to become as popular with your family as it is with ours.

5 green onions, chopped
3/4 cup margarine
2 teaspoons fresh lemon juice
2 teaspoons Dijon mustard
2 teaspoons seasoned salt
1 cup (4 oz.) grated Swiss cheese
1 loaf French bread, cut lengthwise

Heat oven to 350°F.

In medium skillet, sauté onions in margarine over medium heat until onion is soft. Stir in lemon juice, mustard and seasoned salt. Spread mixture on bread halves; sprinkle cheese on top. Put halves back together; wrap in heavy-duty aluminum foil. Bake 15 to 20 minutes or until heated through and cheese is melted.

MINIATURE APPLESAUCE MUFFINS

KRIS (TREVOR) DODDS

Trevor and I love to eat and I really love cooking, probably because I don't get to do it very often. I have found baking is even more enjoyable, especially when the recipe is healthy and sensible.

1 1/4 cups wheat germ or oat bran
1 1/4 cups quick-cooking or old-fashioned oats
1 cup all-purpose flour
1/2 cup packed brown sugar
1 teaspoon baking soda
1 teaspoon cinnamon
1/2 teaspoon salt
1/4 teaspoon nutmeg
1 cup unsweetened applesauce
1/2 cup margarine, melted
1 egg
1 teaspoon vanilla

Heat oven to 400°F. Spray 36 miniature muffin cups with nonstick cooking spray.

In large bowl, mix wheat germ, oats, flour, brown sugar, baking soda, cinnamon, salt and nutmeg. Set aside.

In medium bowl, mix applesauce, margarine, egg and vanilla. With a wooden spoon, stir applesauce mixture into flour mixture just until flour is moistened; stir in raisins and nuts. Batter will be lumpy.

Spoon level tablespoons of batter into muffin cups. Bake 10 to 12 minutes or until muffins are lightly browned. Remove muffins from cups immediately. Serve hot or cool.

Miniature Applesauce Muffins

DECADENT FRENCH TOAST

MARY BET HORAN (TOM SCHERRER'S MOTHER-IN-LAW)

This popular dish works splendid for brunches.

1 cup packed brown sugar
$1/2$ cup butter
2 tablespoons light corn syrup
$1/2$ cup chopped walnuts
1 loaf French or Italian bread, sliced ($1/2$ to
   $3/4$ inch thick)
5 eggs
$1 1/2$ cups milk
1 teaspoon vanilla

In medium saucepan, heat brown sugar, butter, corn syrup and walnuts over medium heat until sugar has melted. Spray 2-quart casserole with nonstick cooking spray. Pour brown sugar mixture into casserole. Place bread slices on brown sugar mixture.

Combine eggs, milk and vanilla in blender; process 15 seconds. Pour egg mixture over bread slices; cover and refrigerate overnight.

Heat oven to 350°F. Bake, uncovered, 30 to 35 minutes or until browned. Invert slices onto platter.

BANANA-BUTTERMILK BUCKWHEAT PANCAKES

JULIA (GLEN) HNATIUK

$1/3$ cup all-purpose flour
$1/3$ cup buckwheat flour
$1/3$ cup whole wheat flour
1 tablespoon sugar
$1/2$ teaspoon salt
$1/2$ teaspoon baking powder
1 egg, beaten
2 tablespoons vegetable oil
1 cup buttermilk
1 ripe banana, mashed
$1/2$ cup pecans, if desired

Heat large skillet to 350°F; spray with nonstick cooking spray.

In large bowl, combine flours, sugar, salt and baking powder. Set aside.

In separate bowl, combine egg, oil and buttermilk; add to flour mixture alternately with mashed banana. Stir just until mixed. Stir in bananas and pecans.

Drop batter by $1/3$ cupfuls onto hot skillet. Adjust heat to medium-high. When bubbles appear on surface of pancake, about 2 to 3 minutes, lift with spatula to see underside has browned. Turn and cook second side until browned, about $1 1/2$ to 2 minutes.

4

Poultry

DIANE'S CHICKEN SPECIALTY

DIANE (KEVIN) WENTWORTH

I enjoy cooking and have a wonderful, appreciative husband who is willing to try anything. One day I concocted this recipe for him; it turned out to be a success.

4 boneless skinless chicken breast halves,
    cut into bite-size pieces
1 yellow onion, thinly sliced
1 (14-oz.) jar marinated artichoke hearts
1 (14-oz.) can sliced peeled tomatoes
6 tablespoons red wine vinegar
1 teaspoon minced garlic
$1/2$ teaspoon salt
$1/2$ teaspoon freshly ground pepper

In large skillet, sauté chicken and onion 5 to 10 minutes or until chicken is no longer pink in center. Add artichoke hearts, tomatoes, vinegar, garlic, salt and pepper. Simmer 30 minutes. Serve over rice, if desired.

CHICKEN POT PIE

LINDA (BOBBY) WADKINS

This dish is easy to make and is often made while Bobby and I travel because it requires such little kitchen space.

1 medium onion, diced
1 tablespoon butter
1 (1-lb.) boneless skinless chicken breast, cooked,
    cut into bite-size pieces
2 ($10^3/4$-oz.) cans cream of potato soup
1 (8.5-oz.) can mixed vegetables
1 (9-inch) prepared pie crust

Heat oven to 350°F.

In large saucepan, sauté onion in butter until tender. Add chicken, soup and vegetables. Put mixture in 2-quart baking dish; cover with pie crust.

Bake 30 minutes or until crust is golden brown.

TEXAS SUSHI

LAURA (GREG) NORMAN

3 cups cooked black beans
2 tablespoons chopped cilantro
1 tablespoon ground cumin
1 jalapeño chile, diced
1 (12-oz.) boneless skinless chicken breast
$1/8$ teaspoon salt, plus more to taste
$1/8$ teaspoon freshly ground pepper, plus more to taste
1 lb. chopped fresh spinach
6 (10-inch) flour tortillas
$1/4$ cup vegetable oil
$1/2$ lb. jalapeño Jack cheese, cut into $1/4$-inch strips
$1/2$ lb. Colby or cheddar cheese, cut into $1/4$-inch strips
1 red bell pepper, cut into matchstick-size strips,
    blanched
1 yellow bell pepper, cut into matchstick-size strips,
    blanched
1 carrot, cut into matchstick-size strips, blanched
1 tablespoon butter, softened

Puree beans in food processor. In medium bowl, combine cilantro, cumin, jalapeño and salt; reserve.

Place chicken on gas grill over medium heat or on charcoal grill 4 to 6 inches from medium coals. Cook, turning occasionally, until chicken is no longer pink in center. Season with salt and pepper. Set aside.

Meanwhile, in large skillet, cook spinach 3 to 4 minutes; let cool. Set aside.

Lightly rub tortillas with oil; place in another large skillet. Cook 2 to 3 seconds or until soft. Spread bean puree over bottom one-third about $1/4$ inch thick. Top with chicken strips, end to end. Sprinkle one line of cheese up each side; top with spinach and one row blanched vegetables. Starting at the full end, roll evenly and firmly. Rub butter on each end to seal tortilla. Wrap in plastic; refrigerate 1 hour or until firm.

Slice into 1-inch pieces; serve at room temperature with salsa.

DIANE'S CHICKEN SPECIALTY

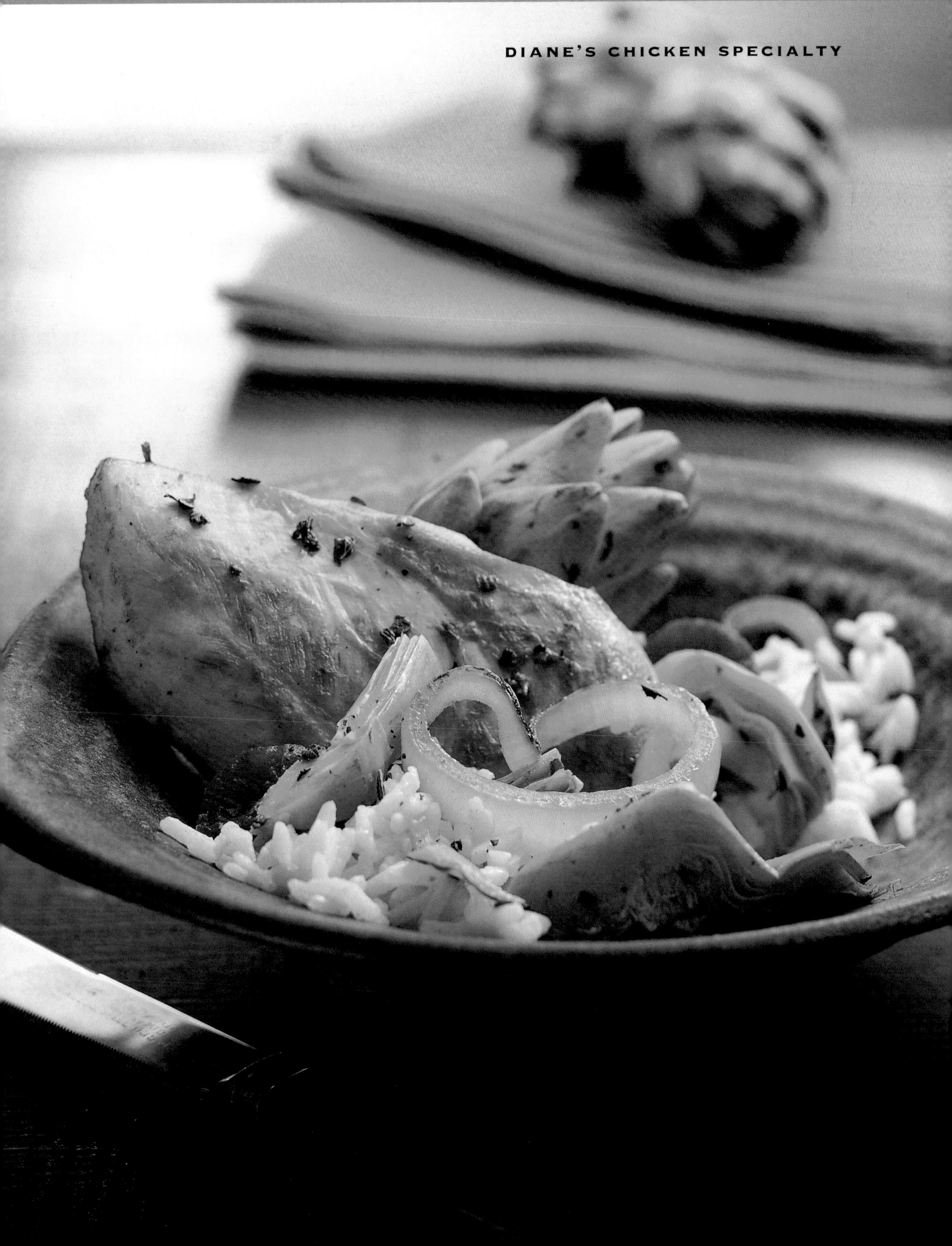

STEVE'S CHICKEN

SALLY (HALE) IRWIN

Hale and I can not believe how simple this dish is to prepare! It became one of our favorites a long time ago and we still enjoy fixing it.

2 boneless skinless chicken breast halves
$1/2$ cup oil-and-vinegar salad dressing

Marinate chicken in salad dressing 1 to 2 hours. Heat grill. Grill chicken on gas grill over medium heat or on charcoal grill 4 to 6 inches from medium coals until chicken juices are clear.

DELICIOUS PAPRIKA CHICKEN

KIM (DICKY) PRIDE

This dish is healthy, low-fat and tastes great! Dicky and I have it often.

2 to 3 boneless skinless chicken breast halves, sliced
    into 2-inch pieces
2 ($10^3/4$-oz.) cans chicken broth
1 garlic clove, minced
1 large onion, thinly sliced
1 or 2 green bell peppers, thinly sliced
1 (14.5-oz.) can diced tomatoes, drained
1 teaspoon salt
$1/2$ teaspoon freshly ground pepper
$1 1/2$ teaspoons paprika
1 cup reduced-fat sour cream

In a large skillet, sauté chicken in $1/2$ cup of the broth about 15 minutes, adding more broth as it cooks away. Remove chicken from skillet, set aside.

Add garlic and onion to skillet, adding broth as needed; cook 15 to 20 minutes or until onion is tender. Add bell peppers, tomatoes, salt, pepper, paprika and chicken. Cook about 45 minutes over medium heat, adding broth or water as liquid cooks away. Mixture should be consistency of stew. Stir in sour cream before serving.

SWISS CHICKEN CUTLETS

TERRI (RICK) FEHR

This recipe makes a delicious "company dinner". Rick and I fix this dish during Christmas as a festive entrée with its bright red and green garnish.

5 boneless skinless chicken breast halves
2 eggs, beaten
1 cup fine dry bread crumbs
$1/4$ cup vegetable oil
3 tablespoons butter
$1/4$ cup all-purpose flour
$1/2$ teaspoon salt
$1/8$ teaspoon freshly ground pepper
$2 1/2$ cups milk
$1/2$ cup dry white wine
1 cup (4 oz.) shredded Swiss cheese

Pound chicken and flatten into $1/4$-inch thickness. Dip chicken in egg, then in crumbs. Heat oil in medium saucepan; cook chicken until brown. Place in 3-quart casserole.

Heat oven to 350°F. In saucepan, melt butter and blend in flour, salt and pepper. Add milk all at once and stir constantly; cook until thick and bubbly. Remove from heat; add wine. Pour sauce over chicken; bake 50 minutes. Sprinkle with cheese. Bake until cheese is melted. Garnish with avocado and tomato slices, if desired.

ROASTED CHICKEN

CHRIS (SCOTT) GUMP

Scott and I eat at a fabulous restaurant, "Cricket's", when we are at the Buick Challenge at Callaway Gardens in Pine Mountain, Georgia. This recipe is a take-off of one of our favorite dishes there.

1 (4- to 5-lb.) whole chicken
1/4 cup vegetable oil
1/2 teaspoon salt
1/2 teaspoon freshly ground pepper
1 teaspoon garlic powder
2 large onions, cut into chunks
3 ribs celery, cut into chunks
3 bay leaves
1/4 cup Worcestershire sauce
1 tablespoon rosemary leaves
1/2 cup white wine

Heat oven to 400°F.

Brush chicken with oil; sprinkle with salt, pepper and garlic on both sides. Place chicken in ungreased 3-quart casserole. Add onions, celery, bay leaves and Worcestershire sauce. Fill casserole halfway with water; add rosemary leaves. Baste; add wine. Bake about 1 hour or until internal temperature reaches 170°F. When chicken browns on top, turn in pan and bake an additional 30 minutes or until golden brown and chicken juices run clear.

BAKED CHICKEN AND GRAVY

BONNIE (STEVE) JONES

This is a tried-and-true favorite for chicken and gravy lovers. Steve and I can't seem to get enough of it.

3- to 31/2-lb. frying chicken pieces, skinned
1/4 cup all-purpose flour
1/4 cup butter, melted
2/3 cup evaporated milk
1 (103/4-oz.) can cream of mushroom soup
1 cup (4 oz.) grated American cheese
1/2 teaspoon salt
1/8 teaspoon freshly ground pepper
1 (1-lb.) can whole onions (2 cups)
1/4 lb. mushrooms, sliced
1/8 teaspoon paprika

Heat oven to 425°F.

Coat chicken with flour. Pour melted butter into 3-quart casserole. Arrange chicken in single layer. Bake, uncovered, 30 minutes. Turn chicken. Bake an additional 15 to 20 minutes or until chicken juices run clear. Reduce temperature to 325°F. Pour off excess fat. In large bowl, combine milk, soup, cheese, salt and pepper; set aside. Add onions and mushrooms to chicken. Pour soup mixture over chicken. Sprinkle with paprika. Cover dish with aluminum foil. Bake 15 to 20 minutes or until cheese is melted and topping begins to brown.

Roasted Chicken

SAUCY CHICKEN

KATHY (CHRIS) PERRY

Chris and I make this frequently for family gatherings and dinner parties. It is always a success.

1 (10³/4-oz.) can cream of mushroom soup

1 cup sour cream

¹/4 to ¹/2 cup dry vermouth (sherry or white wine)

4 boneless skinless chicken breast halves

¹/2 teaspoon salt

¹/2 teaspoon freshly ground pepper

¹/4 cup (1 oz.) freshly grated Parmesan cheese

Heat oven to 350°F.

In large bowl, mix together mushroom soup, sour cream and wine. Pour about one-third of mixture into 2-quart casserole. Sprinkle chicken with salt and pepper; place in casserole. Pour remaining soup mixture over chicken. Sprinkle cheese over top. Cover with aluminum foil. Bake 1 hour or until chicken juices run clear.

CHICKEN BREASTS IN WINE SAUCE

MOLLY (LEE) RINKER

With our family's busy schedule, this dish comes in handy when time is a factor and when we need something the whole family will eat.

¹/2 cup butter

6 boneless skinless chicken breast halves

2 (10³/4-oz.) can cream of chicken soup

2 (8-oz.) cans water chestnuts, sliced

2 (4-oz.) cans button mushrooms

³/4 teaspoon thyme

1¹/2 cups sauterne cooking wine

Heat oven to 350°F.

In medium skillet, melt butter over medium-high heat. Cook chicken until browned. Place chicken into 3-quart casserole. In medium bowl, combine soup, water chestnuts, mushrooms, thyme and wine; mix well. Pour mixture over chicken. Bake 1 hour or until chicken juices run clear.

TURKEY DIVAN BY BERT ELMORE

DEBBYE (BRIAN) WATTS

Bert hosted a dinner at her house for both families the Thursday before Brian and I were married. This was the casserole she prepared and everyone loved it.

MAIN INGREDIENTS

1 cup broccoli florets, cooked

³/4 cup (3 oz.) freshly grated Parmesan cheese

1 lb. sliced turkey

SAUCE

¹/4 cup margarine

3 tablespoons all-purpose flour

2 cups milk

¹/2 teaspoon nutmeg

¹/2 teaspoon Worcestershire sauce

¹/2 teaspoon salt

¹/2 teaspoon freshly ground pepper

¹/2 cup mayonnaise

¹/2 cup heavy cream

Heat oven to 350°F.

Layer broccoli, ¹/2 cup of the cheese and turkey in 3-quart casserole.

In medium saucepan, combine margarine, flour, milk, nutmeg, Worcestershire, salt, pepper, mayonnaise and cream. Whisk over medium heat until thickened. Pour sauce over turkey; sprinkle with remaining ¹/4 cup cheese.

Bake 30 minutes or until bubbly and brown.

CHICKEN POT PIE

JENNIFER (TOM) SCHERRER

Tom is a meat-and-potato type of guy and one day I decided to make something a little different. Hesitantly, I asked him what he thought—I received much praise, to my surprise, and I have served this hundreds of times since.

3 boneless skinless chicken breast halves
2 teaspoons celery salt
2 chicken bouillon cubes
1 (10-oz.) pkg. frozen sliced carrots, thawed
1 (10-oz.) pkg. frozen peas, thawed
1 to 3 tablespoons all-purpose flour
1 box frozen puff pastry shells

In large pot, cover chicken with water. Add celery salt and bouillon. Simmer over medium heat about 45 minutes or until chicken juices run clear. Remove chicken from broth.

In another large pot, warm carrots and peas; drain and set aside.

Discard one-half of broth. Heat remaining broth to a simmer; stir in flour, one tablespoon at a time, stirring constantly, until sauce is consistency of gravy.

Heat oven to 350°F. Chop chicken; add to gravy. Add carrots and peas; mix well. Bake pastry shells according to package directions. Remove pastry shell tops; fill with hot chicken mixture. Bake 1 hour.

BLACK BEAN CHICKEN ENCHILADAS

MOLLY (DAVID) SUTHERLAND

I won David's heart with this recipe which I modified from The Cerebral Palsy Guild Cookbook, 1992. I first made it for him the day he made it through Qualifying-school; it has been a hit since then.

ENCHILADAS
3/4 lb. boneless skinless chicken breast halves
4 to 5 thick slices bacon
2 garlic cloves, crushed
1 1/2 cups picante sauce
1 (16-oz.) can black beans, drained
1 red bell pepper, chopped
1 teaspoon ground cumin
1/4 teaspoon salt
1/2 cup green onions, sliced
12 (6- to 7-inch) flour tortillas
1 cup (4 oz.) shredded Monterey Jack cheese
1/4 cup (1 oz.) shredded cheddar cheese

TOPPINGS
Chopped tomatoes
Sour cream
Olives
Avocado slices

Heat oven to 350°F. Spray baking sheet with nonstick cooking spray.

Cut chicken into thin strips. In large skillet, cook bacon until crisp; crumble. Reserve 2 tablespoons drippings. Cook chicken and garlic in drippings, stirring constantly, until chicken is no longer pink in center. Add 1/2 cup of the picante sauce, beans, red pepper, cumin and salt. Simmer until thickened, about 7 to 8 minutes.

Stir in green onions and reserved bacon bits. Spoon heaping 1/4 cup bean mixture down center of each tortilla. Top each with 1 tablespoon cheese. Roll up; place enchilada, seam side down, on baking sheet. Spoon remaining 1/2 cup picante sauce evenly over enchiladas. Bake 15 minutes; top with remaining cheese. Return to oven; bake an additional 3 minutes or until cheese is melted.

HONEY DIJON CHICKEN

MELANIE (PHIL) TATAURANGI

As you can see, this recipe is easy to prepare and has been a favorite for Phil and I since we first tried it.

3/4 cup honey
1/2 cup Dijon mustard
2 garlic cloves, minced
8 chicken pieces
1/2 onion, cut into wedges

Heat oven to 375°F.

In small bowl, mix honey, mustard and garlic. Place chicken pieces and onion into 2-quart baking dish. Pour honey-mustard mixture over chicken. Bake 1 hour and 15 minutes or until chicken is no longer pink in center and juices run clear.

MICROWAVE ONION AND CHEESE CHICKEN

BONNIE (LARRY) MIZE

This recipe is one of Larry's most requested dishes. I take pleasure in making it because it is so easy to prepare and I know it will bring rave reviews.

4 tablespoons butter
1 teaspoon seasoned salt
1 teaspoon freshly ground pepper
6 boneless skinless chicken breast halves
1/2 lb. fresh mushrooms, sliced
1 (3-oz.) can french fried onions
3/4 cup (3 oz.) shredded Monterey Jack cheese

In microwave-safe dish, heat butter 30 seconds or until melted. Add salt and pepper. Roll chicken in butter mixture. Arrange chicken in 12x7 1/2-inch baking dish. Cover with parchment paper; microwave on High power 5 to 6 minutes. Turn chicken over; top with mushrooms. Cover and continue cooking on High power an additional 4 minutes. Sprinkle with onions and cheese. Cover and cook on high power 2 to 3 minutes or until cheese is bubbly.

Honey Dijon Chicken

BEST YET CHICKEN

CATHY (MARK) WIEBE

At our house we really like easy recipes such as this one. This is a dish that even Mark and the kids can make without any difficulty.

8 boneless skinless chicken breast halves
8 slices Swiss cheese
1 (10^3/$_4$-oz.) can cream of mushroom soup
^{1}/$_4$ cup white wine
2 cups herb stuffing mix
^{1}/$_4$ cup butter, melted

Heat oven to 350°F.

In 3-quart casserole, arrange chicken over bottom. Top with Swiss cheese.

In small bowl, combine soup and wine. Stir in stuffing; mix well. Spread over chicken. Drizzle with melted butter.

Bake, uncovered, 1 hour.

CHICKEN PICCATA

LISA (STEWART) CINK

I originally got this great recipe from Southern Living Magazine.

6 boneless skinless chicken breasts halves
^{1}/$_3$ cup all-purpose flour
1 teaspoon salt
^{1}/$_4$ teaspoon freshly ground pepper
^{1}/$_4$ cup butter
^{1}/$_4$ cup fresh lemon juice
1 lemon, thinly sliced
2 tablespoons chopped fresh parsley

Heat oven to 350°F.

Place each chicken piece between 2 sheets parchment paper; flatten to ^{1}/$_4$ inch thickness using meat mallet or rolling pin. In medium bowl, combine flour, salt and pepper; dredge chicken in flour mixture.

In large skillet, melt butter over medium heat. Add chicken; cook 3 to 4 minutes on each side or until chicken is no longer pink in center. Remove chicken from skillet, drain on paper towels. Keep warm. Add lemon juice and lemon slices to pan drippings in skillet; cook until thoroughly heated. Pour lemon mixture over chicken. Sprinkle with parsley.

CHICKEN BREASTS WITH CREAMY LINGUINE

DIANNE (TED) SCHULZ

4 boneless skinless chicken breast halves
1 teaspoon salt
1 teaspoon freshly ground pepper
1 teaspoon paprika
2 tablespoons butter
2 tablespoons olive oil
1 onion, cut into ^{1}/$_4$-inch slices
2 garlic cloves, minced
1 cup canned reduced-sodium chicken broth
1 (14.5-oz.) can diced tomatoes, juice reserved
^{1}/$_3$ cup heavy cream
1 (7-oz.) pkg. linguine, broken into 3-inch pieces
1 tablespoon chopped fresh basil
^{1}/$_8$ teaspoon cayenne pepper

Rinse chicken and pat dry. Sprinkle evenly with salt, pepper and paprika.

In large skillet, heat butter and oil. Add chicken; cook on each side 4 minutes. Remove chicken; add onion and garlic. Cook until onion is transparent. Add chicken broth, tomatoes and cream; bring to a boil. Stir in linguine, basil and cayenne; return to a boil. Reduce heat to medium-low.

Add chicken to skillet. Cook, covered, until chicken is no longer pink in center. Transfer chicken to dinner plates. Cook mixture an additional 1 minute. Surround chicken with linguine. Drizzle remaining sauce over chicken.

⑤ MEATS

PORK TENDERLOIN WITH BOURBON MARINADE | *page 63*

VEAL CHOPS | *page 69*

BONNIE'S MARINATED BEEF

BONNIE (LARRY) MIZE

1/3 cup red wine vinegar

2 to 3 tablespoons ketchup

2 tablespoons vegetable oil

1 tablespoon soy sauce

1 tablespoon Worcestershire sauce

1 teaspoon mustard

1 teaspoon salt

1/4 teaspoon freshly ground pepper

2 to 3 garlic cloves, minced

4 (1-inch-thick) top sirloin steaks

In large bowl, combine vinegar, ketchup, oil, soy sauce, Worcestershire sauce, mustard, salt, pepper and garlic; blend well. Pour marinade into large resealable plastic bag. Add steaks; seal bag. Refrigerate several hours or overnight, turning often. When ready to cook, allow steaks to stand 30 minutes at room temperature.

Heat grill. Place steaks on gas grill over medium heat or on charcoal grill 4 to 6 inches from medium coals. Cook 8 to 10 minutes or until of desired doneness, turning once.

FILET MARINADE

SUE (JOEY) SINDELAR

As Joey likes to say, "It's never too cold to grill steaks!" This marinade is used often when we grill—rain, snow, or sun.

2 (1 1/2-lb.) filet mignons

2 garlic cloves, crushed

1 tablespoon olive oil

Heat grill. Rub garlic and oil over both sides of filets; set aside 20 minutes.

Place filets on gas grill over medium heat or on charcoal grill 4 to 6 inches from medium coals. Cook 6 to 8 minutes, turning once, until filets are slightly pink in center.

VEAL SCHNITZEL WITH TOMATO AND MOZZARELLA

KRIS (TREVOR) DODDS

Trevor is from a country in Southern Africa called Namibia. Namibia had been occupied by Germany up until 1915, yet the German influence is still prominent today. This dish reminds Trevor of his homeland and is one of our favorites.

6 veal schnitzels (cutlets)

1 egg

2 teaspoons water

1/2 cup finely crushed toasted bread crumbs

1 teaspoon salt

1/2 teaspoon freshly ground pepper, plus more to taste

2 tablespoons freshly grated Parmesan cheese

2 1/2 tablespoons vegetable oil

1 onion, chopped

1 garlic clove, minced

1 (14.5-oz.) can diced tomatoes

1 teaspoon dried basil

2 bay leaves

2 tablespoons chopped fresh parsley

1/4 cup white vermouth

1 teaspoon sugar

1 (8-oz.) pkg. mozzarella cheese, sliced

1/2 teaspoon dried oregano

Heat oven to 300°F. Slice each schnitzel into 2 equal pieces.

In medium bowl, beat egg with water. In another medium bowl, combine bread crumbs, 1/2 teaspoon of the salt, pepper and Parmesan; mix well. Brush veal with egg, then dip in crumbs, coating both sides. Refrigerate 1 hour or until crumbs set.

In large skillet, heat oil over medium-high heat until hot. Cook veal until very lightly browned, turning once. Repeat, adding oil when necessary. Arrange schnitzels in single layer of 3-quart casserole.

Meanwhile, in another large skillet, sauté onion and garlic. Add tomatoes, remaining 1/2 teaspoon salt, basil, bay leaves, parsley, vermouth and sugar; cover and simmer gently 30 minutes. Season with pepper. Discard bay leaves; spoon sauce over veal. Top with mozzarella and sprinkle with oregano. Bake 40 minutes. Add 1 teaspoon water to side of casserole; bake an additional 10 minutes.

APPLE-SAUSAGE RING

LAUREN (JIM) McGOVERN

I always double this recipe when I make it for brunch. It is a great complement to any type of egg dish or quiche. It looks nice and tastes even better.

2 lb. bulk sausage
2 eggs, slightly beaten
1/2 cup milk
1 1/2 cups herb stuffing mix
1/4 cup minced onion
1 cup chopped apples

Heat oven to 350°F. Spray 6-cup Bundt pan with nonstick cooking spray.

In large bowl, combine sausage, eggs, milk, stuffing, onion and apples; mix thoroughly. Press mixture lightly into pan. Invert onto shallow baking dish; bake 1 hour or until sausage is no longer pink in center. Drain and place on serving plate. Add additional chopped apples to center, if desired.

BREAKFAST CASSEROLE

DIANE TRIPLETT (KIRK'S MOM)

This dish works perfectly for those early Christmas mornings when the family is digging into Santa's treasures and you don't want to spend time in the kitchen.

8 slices bread, cubed
2 cups (8 oz.) grated cheddar cheese
1 1/2 lb. cooked linked sausage, cut into pieces
4 eggs
2 1/2 cups milk
1/2 teaspoon salt
3/4 teaspoon dry mustard
1 (10 3/4-oz.) can cream of mushroom soup

Put bread cubes in 3-quart casserole. Cover with cheese and sausage.

In small bowl, combine eggs, 2 cups of the milk, salt and mustard; mix well. Pour mixture over bread, sausage and cheese. Cover with aluminum foil; refrigerate overnight.

Heat oven to 325°F. In small bowl, mix together soup and remaining 1/2 cup milk; pour over mixture in casserole. Bake 1 hour.

CHEESE AND SAUSAGE QUICHE

CATHI (KIRK) TRIPLETT

This dish is extremely versatile. It is tasty and quick for breakfast and can also be heated up for an afternoon snack.

1 (9-inch) unbaked pie shell
3/4 lb. bulk sausage
1/2 cup chopped onion
1/3 cup chopped green onions
2 eggs
1 cup half-and-half
1 1/2 cups (6 oz.) shredded cheddar cheese
1/2 teaspoon salt
1/4 teaspoon garlic salt
1/4 teaspoon freshly ground pepper
1 tablespoon chopped fresh parsley
1 tablespoon all-purpose flour

Heat oven to 400°F. Place pie shell in 9-inch pie pan; prick holes in crust. Bake 5 minutes. Remove from oven and set aside. Reduce oven temperature to 350°F.

In large skillet, cook sausage over medium-high heat until browned. Add onion; sauté 2 to 3 minutes. Remove from heat; drain.

In large mixing bowl, beat eggs and half-and-half at medium speed. Stir in salt, garlic salt, pepper, parsley and flour; beat well.

Crumble sausage, green onions and cheese into pie shell. Top with egg mixture. Bake 30 minutes.

BEEF 'N CHEESE CRESCENT PIE

JULIA (GLEN) HNATIUK

This dish is our "golfers special". It allows Glen and I to enjoy a home-cooked meal while on the road.

1¹/₄ lb. ground beef
¹/₃ cup chopped onion
¹/₃ cup chopped green bell pepper
1 (6-oz.) can tomato sauce
¹/₂ teaspoon garlic salt
¹/₄ teaspoon salt
1 (8-oz.) can refrigerated crescent roll dough
1 egg, slightly beaten
2 cups (8 oz.) shredded cheddar cheese
1 (4-oz.) can chopped green chiles
¹/₂ teaspoon paprika

Heat oven to 375°F. Spray 9-inch pie pan with nonstick cooking spray.

In large skillet, cook beef, onion and bell pepper over medium-high heat until beef is brown and vegetables are tender. Stir in tomato sauce, garlic salt and salt. Reduce heat to a simmer; cook 5 minutes. Press dough into pan.

In large bowl, combine egg and 1¹/₂ cups of the cheese; spread over crust. Spread with green chiles. Spoon beef mixture over chiles; sprinkle with remaining ¹/₂ cup cheese and paprika.

Bake 20 to 25 minutes or until cheese is melted.

PORK TENDERLOIN WITH BOURBON MARINADE

DIANE (FUZZY) ZOELLER

¹/₄ cup bourbon
¹/₄ cup soy sauce
¹/₄ cup packed brown sugar
3 garlic cloves, minced
¹/₄ cup Dijon mustard
¹/₂ teaspoon salt
¹/₄ cup vegetable oil
1 tablespoon Worcestershire sauce
2 (1-lb.) pork tenderloins

In 3-quart casserole, combine bourbon, soy sauce, brown sugar, garlic, mustard, salt, oil and Worcestershire sauce. Place pork in marinade; turn to coat. Cover and refrigerate 1 hour or up to 12 hours. Remove pork from marinade; discard marinade.

Heat grill. Place pork on gas grill over medium heat or on charcoal grill 4 to 6 inches from medium coals. Cook about 6 minutes; turn tenderloin ¹/₄ turn. Cook another 6 minutes; turn another ¹/₄ turn. Continue cooking until instant-read thermometer reaches 170°F.

Pork Tenderloin with Bourbon Marinade

HAM & CHEESE QUICHE

CATHI (KIRK) TRIPLETT

This dish was served at my restaurant as a lunch special. No surprise that we were always sold out before lunch was even over.

1 (9-inch) unbaked pie shell
1/2 cup (2 oz.) shredded Swiss cheese
1 cup (4 oz.) shredded sharp cheddar cheese
1/2 cup fully cooked diced ham
2 tablespoons honey mustard
5 eggs, beaten
1 1/4 cups half-and-half
1/4 cup chopped green onion
1/4 teaspoon salt

Heat oven to 400°F. Place pie shell in 9-inch pie pan; prick holes in crust. Bake 5 minutes.

Remove pie shell from oven; cover bottom evenly with cheese and ham. Reduce oven temperature to 350°F.

In large bowl, combine mustard, eggs, half-and-half, onion and salt; pour over cheese and ham.

Bake 40 to 45 minutes or until quiche begins to brown.

BEEF TENDERLOIN

PAM (DOUG) TEWELL

This recipe is actually from Jana (Mark) Hayes, but it is our favorite meat entreé.

1 tablespoon salt
1 tablespoon freshly ground pepper
1 tablespoon soy sauce
1 tablespoon seasoned salt, if desired
1 (3- to 5-lb.) beef tenderloin

Heat broiler. In small bowl, combine salt, pepper, soy sauce and seasoned salt; mix well. Rub mixture over meat. Place meat on aluminum foil; broil 7 minutes on each side.

Heat oven to 350°F. Wrap meat in foil; bake an additional 15 minutes. Slice meat into 1-inch slices and place in microwave-safe dish. Pour drippings over meat. Microwave on High 4 minutes.

SMOKED BRISKET

NANCY LEONARD (JUSTIN'S MOM)

Justin and his friends always enjoy this brisket. I always serve it at my Texas barbecue dinners.

4 to 6 lb. fresh beef brisket
1 bottle liquid smoke
1/2 teaspoon salt
1/2 teaspoon garlic salt
1/2 teaspoon celery salt
2 onions, chopped
7 tablespoons Worcestershire sauce
6 oz. Kraft barbecue sauce

Place brisket in shallow baking dish. Pour liquid smoke over brisket; sprinkle with salts and cover with onion. Cover and refrigerate overnight. Remove brisket from marinade; discard marinade. Sprinkle brisket with Worcestershire sauce. Evenly coat with barbecue sauce.

Heat oven to 275°F. Cover with aluminum foil. Bake 5 hours. Uncover; bake an additional 1 hour.

SWEDISH MEATBALLS

MIA (JESPER) PARNEVIK

This is Jesper's most requested dish. He absolutely loves it . . . as do I.

1 lb. ground beef
1 to 2 onions, chopped
1/2 teaspoon freshly ground pepper
1/2 teaspoon ground white pepper
1/2 teaspoon salt
1 egg
1/3 cup heavy cream
1 tablespoon vegetable oil

In large bowl, mix beef with onions, pepper and salt. Mix in egg and cream. Form into 1-inch round balls.

In medium skillet, heat oil over medium-high heat until hot. Add meatballs; cook until beef is no longer pink in center. Serve with mashed potatoes and Swedish lingonberries, if desired.

GREG TWIGG'S HEAVENLY RIBS

TERESA (GREG) TWIGG

This recipe has been served to over 300 pro golfers on the PGA TOUR and has been one of their favorites. I hope you enjoy them—I'm sure they will lower your score.

2 lb. pork baby-back ribs (4 racks)
1/8 teaspoon salt
1 teaspoon garlic powder
1/2 teaspoon freshly ground pepper
1/4 cup packed brown sugar
1/4 cup maple syrup
1/4 cup Worcestershire sauce
1/4 cup honey
1/2 cup barbecue sauce

Soak hickory chips in water 1 hour; drain. Heat oven to 350°F. Sprinkle ribs with salt, garlic powder and pepper; place in disposable roasting pan.

Pat 1 tablespoon of the brown sugar onto each rack of ribs; pour syrup, Worcestershire sauce and honey over ribs.

Stack ribs on top of each other; wrap stack in aluminum foil. Bake 1 hour.

Heat grill. Add hickory chips to grill.

Place ribs on grill; brush with barbecue sauce. Cook ribs on gas grill over medium heat or on charcoal grill 4 to 6 inches from medium coals 30 minutes, turning once until ribs are golden brown.

FLANK STEAK MARINADE

TERRI (RICK) FEHR

This is a long-time family recipe and is a much beloved dish by Rick. It is delicious especially accompanied with hot garlic bread.

1 cup soy sauce
4 garlic cloves, minced
1 teaspoon freshly ground pepper
1 teaspoon ground ginger
1/2 cup packed brown sugar
4 green onions, thinly sliced
1 (3- to 5-lb.) flank steak

In large resealable plastic bag, combine soy sauce, garlic, pepper, ginger, brown sugar and onions; reserve ¼ of the marinade. Add steak to bag; seal bag. Refrigerate 10 to 12 hours. Remove steak from marinade; discard marinade.

Heat grill. Place steak on gas grill over medium-high heat or on charcoal grill 4 to 6 inches from medium coals. Cook 7 minutes; turn and baste with reserved marinade. Cook an additional 5 to 7 minutes or until meat is no longer pink in center.

YORKSHIRE PUDDING

MELISSA (TOM) LEHMAN

Tom and I have found the perfect combination for a meal is this Yorkshire pudding and roast beef or prime rib. It is a meal we love to make together.

1/3 cup roast beef or bacon
      drippings
3 eggs
1 cup milk
1 cup all-purpose flour
1/2 teaspoon salt

Heat oven to 425°F. Pour drippings into 9-inch square pan. Warm pan and drippings in oven while preparing pudding.

In large bowl, beat eggs at low speed. Add milk, flour and salt; beat at medium speed 30 seconds.

Remove pan from oven; pour egg mixture into pan. Bake 12 minutes or until golden brown. Serve warm.

RAYMOND'S SPICY CHILI

MARIA (RAYMOND) FLOYD

We have found the chili tastes even better the next day—that is if there are any leftovers.

^{1}/4 cup vegetable oil

3 lb. boneless beef shank, cut into ^{1}/2-inch cubes

2 garlic cloves, minced

2 onions, chopped

1^1/2 cups tomato sauce

1 (12-oz.) can beer

3 tablespoons chili powder

^{3}/4 teaspoon ground cumin

1 teaspoon paprika

1 teaspoon salt

^{1}/4 teaspoon freshly ground pepper

^{1}/4 teaspoon cayenne pepper

Heat oil in large pot. Cook beef over low heat 8 to 10 minutes or until almost brown.

Add garlic and onions; simmer, covered, 8 minutes. Add tomato sauce and beer; simmer, covered, 12 minutes.

In small bowl, combine seasonings; add to meat mixture. Cover and cook over low heat 1 hour and 30 minutes or until meat breaks apart with fork. Store overnight in refrigerator. Heat and serve.

WILD ROSCOE DUCK

JENNIFER (SCOTT) McCARRON

After one of his first duck hunts, Scott cleaned the birds, prepared the dish and served it with mashed potatoes and asparagus as a romantic dinner for the two of us. He even did the dishes!

1 oven cooking bag

1 pkg. brown gravy mix

^{1}/4 cup all-purpose flour

1 teaspoon salt

2 tablespoons sugar

2 tablespoons plum jam

1 (3-oz.) can
    guava/strawberry juice*

1^1/2 cups hot water

4 to 6 boneless skinless duck breasts, halved

Heat oven to 350°F.

In oven bag, combine gravy mix, flour, salt and sugar. Add jam, juice and water; mix well. Place breasts in bag, breast side up. Place in shallow roasting pan; seal according to package directions. Cut three small slits in top of bag. Bake 2 hours. Place breasts on serving dish; pour sauce into gravy boat.

TIP *Can substitute with orange juice.

MARINADE FOR PORK TENDERLOIN

CATHY (MARK) WIEBE

Mark is king of the barbecue at our house and this is his favorite to make . . . and our favorite to eat.

^{1}/2 cup olive oil

^{1}/2 cup soy sauce

^{1}/4 cup balsamic vinegar

1 shallot, chopped

^{1}/2 teaspoon dried basil

^{1}/2 teaspoon dried oregano

In large bowl, combine olive oil, soy sauce, vinegar, shallot, basil and oregano; mix well. Add tenderloins; refrigerate overnight.

POT ROAST

CAROLYN (ED) DOUGHERTY

This dinner is perfect for a hearty "meat and potatoes meal" when served with mashed potatoes. We love it!

1 (4-lb.) boneless beef roast
2 tablespoons olive oil
1 cup water
1 teaspoon garlic powder
$1/2$ teaspoon dry mustard
$1/2$ teaspoon freshly ground pepper
$1/4$ cup soy sauce
1 tablespoon honey
1 tablespoon vinegar
1 teaspoon celery seed
$1 1/2$ tablespoons cornstarch

Heat oven to 350°F.

In Dutch oven, brown roast in 2 tablespoons oil. In medium bowl, combine water, garlic powder, dry mustard, pepper, soy sauce, honey, vinegar, celery seed and cornstarch; mix well. Pour over meat.

Bake, covered, 2 hours or until tender, turning occasionally.

SPANISH PORK CHOPS

BYRON NELSON

This dish is simple and delicious. Along with a green salad, it completes one of the favorite meals at my house.

6 ($1 1/2$-inch-thick) pork chops
1 onion, sliced
1 green bell pepper, sliced
2 ribs celery, sliced
3 carrots, sliced lengthwise
6 potatoes, sliced
1 ($10 3/4$-oz.) can tomato soup
1 soup-can water
$1/8$ teaspoon hot pepper sauce
$1/2$ teaspoon salt
$1/2$ teaspoon freshly ground pepper

Heat oven to 350°F.

In large skillet, cook pork over medium-high heat 1 to 2 minutes, turning once, or until brown. Place pork in 2-quart casserole; top with onion, bell pepper, celery, carrots, potatoes, soup, water, hot pepper sauce, salt and pepper. Bake, covered, 1 to 2 hours or until tender, turning occasionally.

VEAL CHOPS

SALLY (HALE) IRWIN

Hale and I really like this sauce and have found it is exceptional not only on meat, but fish and chicken as well. It is even good cold.

2 ($1 1/2$-inch-thick) veal chops
$1 1/8$ teaspoons freshly ground pepper
$1 1/8$ teaspoons seasoned salt
2 tablespoons tarragon vinegar
$1/2$ teaspoon dried tarragon
$1/2$ cup mayonnaise
1 pasteurized egg yolk

Heat grill. Season chops with $1/8$ teaspoon each of the salt and pepper. Place veal on gas grill over medium heat or on charcoal grill 4 to 6 inches from medium coals. Cook, turning once, until instant-read thermometer reaches 170°F.

In medium saucepan, combine 1 teaspoon pepper, 1 teaspoon salt, vinegar, tarragon, mayonnaise and egg yolk. Heat over low heat; beat with wire whisk until warm. Serve over chops.

Veal Chops

MIKE'S FAVORITE KETCHUP BURGERS

JUDY (MIKE) BRISKY

This recipe did not have a name when it was passed down to me from Mike's mother, but we have named it appropriately because Mike adores them!

1^{1}/$_{2}$ lb. ground beef
^{1}/$_{2}$ cup bread crumbs
2 tablespoons Worcestershire
   sauce
^{1}/$_{2}$ cup chopped green bell
   pepper
1 onion, chopped
1 egg
2 tomatoes, chopped
^{1}/$_{4}$ cup parsley
1 tablespoon minced garlic
2 cups ketchup
^{1}/$_{2}$ teaspoon salt
^{1}/$_{2}$ teaspoon freshly ground pepper
Water
1 teaspoon all-purpose flour

In large bowl, combine beef, bread crumbs, Worcestershire sauce, bell pepper, onion, egg, tomatoes, parsley and garlic. Form mixture into 8 to 10 patties. Brown patties in skillet; remove and set aside.

Cook off water remaining in skillet. Replace patties, cover and steam over low heat 30 minutes. Remove again. Brown remaining drippings. Add ketchup, salt and pepper; brown again. Add water, 1 teaspoon at a time, to create gravy, stirring constantly until smooth. Add patties and simmer until heated through.

SAUSAGE AND NEW POTATOES (WITH PASTA)

CATHI (KIRK) TRIPLETT

This is the perfect dinner after a long, cold day on the links.

Pasta of choice
6 tablespoons olive oil
^{3}/$_{4}$-lb. spicy Italian sausage, casings removed
16 new potatoes, washed, sliced (^{1}/$_{4}$ inch thick)
2 onions, coarsely chopped
2 garlic cloves, finely chopped
1 (28-oz.) can whole tomatoes
1^{1}/$_{2}$ tablespoons dried oregano
1 tablespoon double concentrate tomato paste
1 teaspoon sugar
^{3}/$_{4}$ teaspoon salt
^{1}/$_{8}$ teaspoon freshly ground pepper

Cook pasta according to package directions.

In large skillet, heat oil over medium-high heat until hot; crumble in sausage. Add potatoes, onion and garlic; sauté 7 to 10 minutes or until sausage and potatoes begin to brown. Discard fat. Add tomatoes, breaking them up with your hands. Stir in oregano, tomato paste, sugar, salt and pepper. Boil 15 minutes or until thick. Serve over cooked pasta.

DUCKS

CISSYE (JIM) GALLAGHER

A fresh fruit salad (page 30) compliments this hearty dinner.

3 ducks
1 pkg. shrimp and crab boil
1 teaspoon seasoning salt
^{1}/$_{2}$ cup each butter, fresh lemon juice
6 thick slices bacon, cooked, halved

Heat oven to 500°F. In large pot, boil ducks in water with shrimp boil and salt until tender. Remove from water; drain. In small skillet, heat butter and lemon juice over low heat until hot.

Place ducks in 3-quart casserole. Pour butter and lemon mixture over each duck. Place 2 strips bacon across each duck. Bake until bacon is crisp. Serve with Spoon Bread (page 42).

ALOHA PORK

TERRI (RICK) FEHR

This wonderfully flavorful dish was introduced to Rick and I at our engagement party dinner. Rick's mother passed the recipe on to me and I often serve it with Mushroom-Rice Pilaf (page 102).

MARINADE
1/4 cup soy sauce
3 tablespoons sherry
1 garlic clove, crushed
1/2 teaspoon cinnamon
1/2 teaspoon thyme

MEAT
1 (3- to 5-lb.) pork tenderloin

SAUCE
2/3 cup peach or apricot preserves
1/4 cup chili sauce
1 (8-oz.) can sliced water chesnuts
1 cup hot water

Combine soy sauce, sherry, garlic, cinnamon and thyme in large roasting pan. Reserve ¼ of the marinade. Add pork; refrigerate 2 to 3 hours.

Heat oven to 325°F. Remove pork from marinade; discard marinade. Bake pork 1 hour or until internal temperature reaches 170°F. Slice pork into ¼-inch-thick medallions; arrange on serving platter. Keep warm.

Combine preserves, chili sauce, water chesnuts and hot water in saucepan; stir in reserved marinade. Bring to a boil, stirring occasionally. Pour sauce over medallions before serving.

SHEPHERD'S PIE

CATHI (KIRK) TRIPLETT

If you ever stop in a pub in England or Scotland during the British Open, chances are you will find this dish on the lunch menu. It is most satisfying on a cold and rainy day.

1 1/2 lb. potatoes, peeled
2 to 3 tablespoons milk
2 tablespoons margarine
1 teaspoon salt
1 teaspoon freshly ground pepper
2 tablespoons shortening
1 onion, peeled, diced
3/4 lb. minced beef
1 tablespoon all-purpose flour
1 beef bouillon cube
1 cup water

Spray 9-inch pie pan with nonstick cooking spray.

Heat oven to 425°F. Boil potatoes until tender; mash with milk, margarine and ½ teaspoon each of the salt and pepper. Set aside.

In medium skillet, melt shortening over medium heat; cook onion in shortening. Add beef and cook until meat is brown. Sprinkle in flour; stir well. Add bouillon and water; mix well. Simmer 10 minutes. Stir in remaining ½ teaspoon each salt and pepper.

Spread meat mixture in pie plate; spread potato evenly over beef. Smooth with knife or mark surface with fork. Sprinkle top with parsley, if desired. Bake about 30 minutes or until potato is golden brown. Serve hot.

SEAFOOD

SAVORY SALMON STEAKS

KAREN (BRANDEL) CHAMBLEE

After being on the road for three weeks, Brandel and I were looking forward to some home cooking. This quick and easy dish was just what we were looking for. Brandel gives it four stars!

MARINADE
3 tablespoons Dijon mustard
3 tablespoons soy sauce
3 tablespoons packed brown
  sugar
3 tablespoons safflower oil
1 teaspoon prepared
  horseradish

FISH
4 salmon steaks

In small bowl, combine mustard, soy sauce, brown sugar, oil and horseradish. Brush fish with half of the marinade; reserve remaining half. Refrigerate, covered, up to 6 hours.

Heat grill. Grill fish 5 minutes on gas grill over medium heat or on charcoal grill 4 to 6 inches from medium coals. Turn and brush with remaining marinade. Grill until fish just begins to flake. Serve hot or at room temperature.

BREADED ORANGE ROUGHY

KRIS (TREVOR) DODDS

Both Trevor and I love the mild taste of orange roughy. This dish is prepared often at our house.

1 tablespoon dry sherry
1 tablespoon fresh lemon juice
3 tablespoons seasoned bread crumbs
2 tablespoons freshly grated Parmesan cheese
$1/4$ teaspoon garlic powder
$1/4$ teaspoon onion powder
1 lb. orange roughy fillets

Heat oven to 400°F. Spray 9-inch square pan with nonstick cooking spray.

In shallow bowl, mix sherry and lemon juice. In another shallow bowl, combine bread crumbs, cheese, garlic powder and onion powder. Dip fish in sherry mixture; coat with bread crumb mixture. Place fish in pan. Bake, uncovered, 20 to 25 minutes or until fish just begins to flake.

BARBARA'S SHRIMP DISH

MOLLY (LEE) RINKER

I chose this dish as my birthday meal every year while growing up. It's a great one.

1 cup (4 oz.) shredded Parmesan cheese
2 tablespoons fresh lemon juice
$3/4$ cup chopped chives and parsley
1 tablespoon olive oil
1 lb. sliced mushrooms
$1/2$ cup butter
2 garlic cloves, minced
2 lb. shelled, deveined uncooked medium shrimp
1 cup Caesar croutons

In large bowl, combine cheese, lemon juice and chive mixture; set aside.

In large skillet, heat olive oil over medium-high heat until hot; sauté mushrooms. Set aside. In another large skillet heat butter until melted. Add garlic; sauté 1 minute.

Add shrimp to skillet; sauté until shrimp turn pink. Stir in cheese mixture, mushrooms and garlic. Warm and serve quickly over rice, if desired.

SPICY CHILE SHRIMP

SELENA (FRANK) NOBILO

1 lb. shelled, deveined uncooked medium shrimp
1 onion, peeled
2 garlic cloves, peeled
4 jalapeño chiles, seeded
2 tablespoons fresh lemon juice
1 tablespoon vegetable oil
Soy sauce
Fresh coriander
White rice

Peel and clean shrimp.

In blender, combine onion, garlic and chiles; chop finely. Do not puree. Stir in lemon juice.

In wok, heat vegetable oil over medium-high heat until hot. Stir in chile mixture. Add shrimp; sauté about 10 minutes or until shrimp turn pink. Add soy sauce. Garnish with fresh coriander. Serve with white rice.

SAUTEED SEA SCALLOPS WITH MUSTARD SAUCE

TIM FINCHEM (PGA TOUR COMMISSIONER)

1 1/2 lb. sea scallops
1 teaspoon salt
1 teaspoon freshly ground pepper
3 tablespoons olive oil
2 large shallots, minced
1/2 cup dry white wine
2/3 cup water
1/4 cup Dijon mustard
1/4 cup chilled butter, cut into small pieces
4 green onions, cut diagonally into 1/4-inch slices
    (about 2 tablespoons)

Rinse scallops and pat dry; sprinkle with 1/2 teaspoon of the salt and 1/2 teaspoon of the pepper. Heat olive oil in large skillet over medium-high heat until hot. Sauté scallops in oil 1 to 2 minutes on each side until golden and opaque. Set scallops aside on plate; keep warm.

In same skillet, sauté green onions over medium heat, stirring until softened. Add wine; boil 1 minute. Stir in water and mustard; reduce liquid to 1/4 cup. Add butter; swirl until butter is mixed into sauce. Add remaining 1/2 teaspoon salt and remaining 1/2 teaspoon pepper. Pour sauce onto plates; top with green onions and scallops. Serve with rice, if desired.

Shrimp-Caper Mystery

ORANGE ROUGHY ITALIANO

KRIS (TREVOR) DODDS

This recipe, along with the "Breaded Orange Roughy" (page 74) are two of our favorites. Trevor and I love experimenting with different recipes for roughy.

3 tablespoons olive oil
1/2 cup sliced onion
2 1/2 cups thinly sliced zucchini
1 teaspoon dried oregano
1 tomato, chopped
1 lb. orange roughy, cut into serving-size pieces
1/2 teaspoon salt
1/2 teaspoon freshly ground pepper
1/2 cup (2 oz.) shredded provolone cheese

In large skillet, heat oil over medium-high heat until hot. Add onion, zucchini and oregano; sauté 4 minutes. Arrange tomato and fish over vegetables; add salt and pepper. Cover skillet and reduce heat. Simmer 9 minutes.

Sprinkle cheese over fish. Cook, covered, about 1 minute or until cheese is barely melted. Serve immediately.

SHRIMP-CAPER MYSTERY

CATHY (BRIAN) HENNINGER

We originally found this recipe in the Portland Palate Cookbook.

1/4 cup white vinegar
1 teaspoon curry powder
1/2 teaspoon salt
1/2 teaspoon freshly ground pepper
3/4 cup vegetable oil
1 lb. shelled, deveined cooked large shrimp
1/2 cup sliced green onions
4 tablespoons capers

In medium bowl, whisk together vinegar, curry powder, salt and pepper. Slowly stir oil into mixture. Whisk until dressing thickens.

Place shrimp in glass bowl; sprinkle with onions and capers. Pour dressing over shrimp; toss to coat. Cover with aluminum foil. Refrigerate 24 hours. Discard marinade. To serve, drain excess oil; serve with toothpicks.

SAUTEED SEA SCALLOPS
WITH MUSTARD SAUCE

BARBECUE SHRIMP

PATTI (JOHN) INMAN

This recipe is mouthwatering—probably because it is so HOT and so tasty. Don't forget the French bread for dipping.

3/4 cup unsalted butter

Worcestershire sauce

1 tablespoon each cayenne pepper, freshly ground
   pepper

1 1/2 teaspoons each salt, dried thyme, dried rosemary

1/4 teaspoon dried oregano

1 1/2 tablespoons minced garlic

1/2 tablespoon crushed red pepper

2 dozen shelled, deveined uncooked large shrimp

1/2 cup canned reduced-sodium chicken broth

1/4 cup beer

In large skillet, combine 1/2 cup of the butter, Worcestershire sauce, cayenne, pepper, salt, thyme, garlic, red pepper, rosemary and oregano. Blend over high heat. Add shrimp. Cook 1 to 2 minutes or until pink.

Add remaining 1/4 cup butter and broth; heat 1 to 2 minutes or until butter is melted and hot. Add beer; reduce heat to simmer. Stir occasionally.

Spoon 3 to 4 shrimp into bowl; top with sauce. Serve with warm French bread for dipping, if desired.

FISH WITH CITRUS SALSA

JAN (JOHN) COOK

FISH

4 swordfish or Chilean sea bass fillets

Olive oil

CITRUS SALSA

1 tablespoon cilantro

1 jalapeño chile

1 red bell pepper

1 green bell pepper

1 yellow bell pepper

1/2 cup fresh pineapple chunks

1 mango

1 papaya

1 red tomato

Brush fish with olive oil. Heat grill. Cook fish 10 minutes on gas grill over medium heat or on charcoal grill 4 to 6 inches from medium coals. Turn; cook an additional 10 minutes or just until fish flakes easily. Serve with citrus salsa.

For salsa, finely chop cilantro, jalapeno, bell peppers, pineapple, mango, papaya and tomato. Place in large bowl; toss well.

Fish with Citrus Salsa

STEELHEAD

CATHY (BRIAN) HENNINGER

SAUCE
1/2 lb. unsalted butter
2 garlic cloves, halved
1/4 cup soy sauce
2 tablespoons yellow mustard
1 tablespoon Worcestershire
sauce
2 teaspoons ketchup

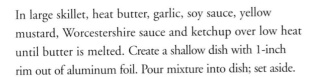

FISH
Fresh Steelhead

In large skillet, heat butter, garlic, soy sauce, yellow
mustard, Worcestershire sauce and ketchup over low heat
until butter is melted. Create a shallow dish with 1-inch
rim out of aluminum foil. Pour mixture into dish; set aside.

Heat grill. Cut fish into serving-size pieces. Baste fish with
sauce. Place fish in foil dish, flesh side down, on grill 4 to 6
inches from medium coals. Sear fish. Turn fish over; sear
other side. Cook until fish flakes easily, basting occasionally.

SHRIMP ETOUFFE

CELESTE GOGEL (MATT'S MOM)

1 1/2 sticks butter
2 to 3 onions, sliced
1 red bell pepper, seeds removed, sliced
4 ribs celery, sliced
1 (14.5-oz.) can diced tomatoes
2 tablespoons fresh lemon juice
1 tablespoon fresh chopped parsley
Dash Worcestershire sauce
2 garlic cloves, minced
1 (10³/4-oz.) can cream of mushroom soup
3 to 4 lb. shelled, deveined uncooked medium shrimp
1/2 cup sherry
White rice, cooked

In large skillet, simmer butter, onions, bell pepper,
celery, tomatoes over low heat 3 hours. Add lemon juice,
parsley, Worcestershire sauce and garlic; blend well. Add
soup, shrimp and sherry. Cook 5 to 10 minutes or until
shrimp turn pink. Serve over white rice.

CRAWFISH MASHED POTATOES

CAROL (PHIL) BLACKMAR

5 Yukon Gold potatoes
3 garlic bulbs
Olive oil
2/3 cup butter
1/2 cup milk
2 tablespoons fresh lemon juice
1 teaspoon Worcestershire sauce
1/2 teaspoon ground white pepper
1/2 teaspoon cayenne pepper
1/2 teaspoon freshly ground pepper
1/2 teaspoon dried thyme
1/2 teaspoon dried rosemary
1 lb. crawfish tails, peeled

Heat oven to 325°F. In Dutch oven, cover potatoes with
water. Boil potatoes until tender. Set aside; keep warm.

Meanwhile, remove tops of garlic bulbs; place on baking
sheet and drizzle with olive oil. Bake 1 hour to 1 hour
and 15 minutes, basting with olive oil every 30 minutes
until garlic is very soft. Remove from oven.

In small saucepan, melt 1/4 cup of the butter; add milk.
Squeeze cooked garlic from cloves into butter. Mash
mixture with spoon.

In large skillet, melt remaining 6 tablespoons butter with
lemon juice, Worcestershire sauce, peppers, thyme and
rosemary. Add crawfish; sauté until crawfish turn pink.
Drain crawfish; set aside.

In Dutch oven, mash potatoes; add garlic mixture and
crawfish. Mix well.

Crawfish Mashed Potatoes

SEAFOOD GUMBO

TILLIE BABIN (STEWART CINK'S GRANDMOTHER)

3/4 cup vegetable oil
2 onions, chopped
4 ribs celery, chopped
2 green bell peppers, chopped
4 cups sliced okra
3/4 cup all-purpose flour
1 (14.5-oz.) can diced tomatoes
1 (1-lb.) can whole tomatoes, sliced
2 quarts water
1 teaspoon sugar
1 teaspoon salt
1 teaspoon freshly ground pepper
1 lb. crabmeat
2 to 3 lb. shelled, deveined uncooked medium shrimp

In large skillet, heat ¼ cup of the oil over medium-high heat until hot. Add onions, celery and bell peppers; sauté until wilted. Add okra; cook an additional 10 minutes.

In separate pan, combine remaining 1/2 cup oil and flour. Cook slowly, stirring often, until color of peanut butter.

In large pot, combine vegetables and tomatoes; add water. Stir in sugar, salt and pepper. Cook over low heat 3 to 5 hours or until vegetables are very tender. Add seafood 20 minutes before serving. Serve with filet powder and cayenne, if desired.

BAKED SEAFOOD CASSEROLE

PENELOPE (LANNY) WADKINS

We always rent a house during the Masters because restaurants get so crowded. This dish always finds its way on the menu of meals for that week—it is too easy NOT to make!

SEAFOOD
12 oz. crabmeat
1 lb. shelled, deveined cooked medium shrimp
1/2 cup diced green bell pepper
1 (2-oz.) jar pimientos, drained
1/2 cup diced onion
1 (4-oz.) can sliced mushrooms, drained
1 cup chopped celery

SEASONING
1 cup mayonnaise
1/2 teaspoon salt
1 cup half-and-half
1/4 teaspoon freshly ground pepper
1 tablespoon Worcestershire sauce
2 cups cooked rice
1/2 cup bread crumbs or 1/2 cup (2 oz.) shredded cheddar cheese

Heat oven to 375°F.

In large bowl, combine crabmeat, shrimp, green bell pepper, pimientos, onion, mushrooms and celery; set aside. In another bowl, combine mayonnaise, salt, half-and-half, pepper, Worcestershire sauce and rice.

Combine crabmeat and mayonnaise mixtures; mix thoroughly. Place mixture in 2-quart casserole; sprinkle with bread crumbs or cheese. Bake, uncovered, 30 minutes.

CRAB CASSEROLE

BARBARA (JACK) NICKLAUS

1/2 lb. fresh mushrooms, sliced
1/4 cup butter melted, plus more for sliced bread
8 slices white bread
8 slices American cheese
1 lb. fresh crab meat
1 onion, chopped
4 eggs, beaten
2 1/2 cups milk
1 teaspoon dry mustard
1 teaspoon salt

Heat oven to 350°F.

In small skillet, sauté mushrooms in butter; set aside. Remove crusts from bread; butter both sides. Place 4 slices bread in bottom of 8-inch square pan. Top with 4 slices of cheese, crab, mushrooms and onions. Add remaining cheese and top with remaining bread slices.

In small bowl, combine eggs, milk, mustard and salt. Mix well; pour over casserole. Cover and soak overnight. Bake, uncovered, 45 to 60 minutes.

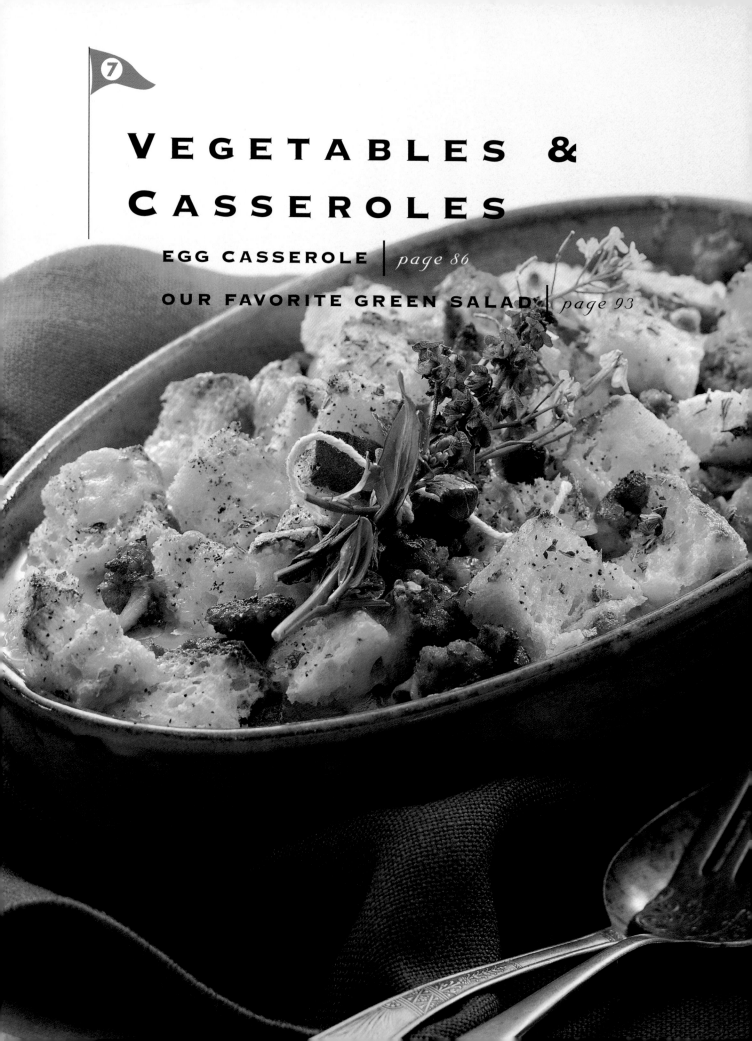

VEGETABLES & CASSEROLES

THAI FRIED NOODLES

KULTIDA WOODS (TIGER'S MOM)

1 lb. Thai rice noodles
1 cup bean sprouts, plus extra for garnish
1/2 cup vegetable oil
1 teaspoon minced garlic
2 eggs
10 shelled, deveined uncooked medium shrimp
1 tablespoon sugar
1 tablespoon oyster sauce
1 teaspoon pounded dried shrimp
1 tablespoon coarsely ground peanuts
1/2 teaspoon chili powder
1 tablespoon chopped green onion
1 tablespoon chopped coriander
2 slices lemon

If using dry noodles, soak in cold water 30 minutes; drain. Place bean sprouts in cold water.

In large skillet, heat oil over medium-high heat until hot. Add garlic; cook 3 minutes or until light brown. Break eggs into skillet. Add noodles; fry until noodles are almost tender. Add shrimp, sugar and oyster sauce; stir together until noodles are tender and shrimp turn pink.

Drain bean sprouts; add to egg mixture and fry until bean sprouts are cooked. Place on serving plate with raw bean sprouts on side. Sprinkle with dried shrimp, peanuts and chili powder. Top with green onion, fresh coriander and lemon. Serve hot.

BAKED BEAN CASSEROLE

CATHY (MARK) WIEBE

1/2 lb. thick sliced bacon, cut up
1 1/2 lb. ground beef
2 onions, chopped
2 (14-oz.) cans pork and beans
1 (14.5-oz.) can stewed tomatoes
3/4 cup packed brown sugar
1 teaspoon chili powder
1 teaspoon celery salt

Heat oven to 300°F.

In medium skillet, cook bacon over medium-high heat until crisp. Remove from skillet; discard bacon fat. Add ground beef and onions. Cook until beef is no longer pink in center. Combine beef with beans, tomatoes, brown sugar, chili powder and celery salt; add bacon.

Spoon mixture into 2 (1 1/2-quart) casseroles. Bake, uncovered, 2 hours.

SAVORY GREEN BEANS WITH SHALLOTS

LISA (STEWART) CINK

This recipe is taken from Feast of Eden, a gift from Pebble Beach one year (Junior League of Monterey County).

4 lean slices bacon
1/2 cup shallots
2 tablespoons herb vinegar
1 teaspoon Dijon mustard
1 lb. fresh green beans, cut French style
Salt to taste
Freshly ground pepper to taste
2 tablespoons chopped chives

In large skillet, fry bacon until crisp. Drain bacon; crumble into small bits. Sauté shallots in bacon fat until tender; do not brown. Stir in vinegar and mustard; set aside.

Cook beans in boiling water 5 to 6 minutes or until tender. Drain well. Add beans to skillet; toss well. Season with salt and pepper. Sprinkle with chives.

HARRIET'S POTATO CASSEROLE

PAM (DOUG) TEWELL

This is truly a family favorite and is now required at almost every holiday meal.

2 lb. frozen hash browns, thawed, drained
$3/4$ cup margarine, melted
1 teaspoon salt
$1/2$ teaspoon freshly ground pepper
2 tablespoons minced onion
1 ($10^3/4$-oz.) can cream of chicken soup
2 cups sour cream
2 cups (8 oz.) shredded cheddar cheese
2 cups corn flakes, crushed

Heat oven to 350°F. Spray 2-quart casserole with nonstick cooking spray.

In large bowl, combine hash browns, $1/2$ cup of the margarine, salt, pepper, onion, soup, sour cream and cheese; mix well. Spread mixture in casserole.

In medium bowl, stir together remaining $1/4$ cup margarine and corn flakes; pour over potatoes.

Bake, uncovered, 45 minutes to 1 hour or until browned and bubbly.

SPICY CHICKEN AND SPAGHETTI CASSEROLE

JULIA (GLEN) HNATIUK

This is a favorite served to us by a family that hosted us during a tournament in Wichita, Kansas. We have found it is perfect for serving large crowds.

2 (14.5-oz.) cans reduced-sodium chicken broth
1 (12-oz.) pkg. thin spaghetti
1 tablespoon olive oil
1 onion, chopped
1 green bell pepper, chopped
4 cups cooked shredded chicken
1 (1-lb.) loaf process cheese spread, diced
$1 1/2$ (28-oz.) cans whole tomatoes, undrained
1 can English peas, drained

Heat oven to 350°F.

In large saucepan, bring chicken broth to a boil. Add spaghetti; cook according to package directions. Drain; set aside.

In large skillet, heat olive oil over medium-high heat until hot; sauté onion and bell pepper until tender. Stir in spaghetti, chicken, cheese, tomatoes and peas; mix well. Spread mixture in 3-quart casserole.

Bake, uncovered, 30 minutes.

EGG CASSEROLE

PAM (DOUG) TEWELL

6 slices bread, crusts trimmed, cubed
1 lb. sausage, cooked, drained, crumbled
6 to 10 eggs, beaten
2 cups (8 oz.) shredded cheddar cheese
2 cups milk
$1 1/2$ teaspoons salt
$1/2$ teaspoon freshly ground pepper
1 teaspoon dry mustard

Spray 3-quart casserole with nonstick cooking spray.

Line bottom of casserole with bread slices and sausage. In large bowl, combine eggs, cheese, milk, salt, pepper and mustard; mix well. Pour mixture over bread and sausage. Refrigerate overnight.

Heat oven to 350°F. Bake, uncovered, 30 minutes.

Egg Casserole

OVERNIGHT EGGS

TRACY (BRIAN) CLAAR

*This dish has become a part of our Christmas morning rituals.
It is a family tradition that everyone enjoys taking part in.*

6 eggs
2 cups milk
1 teaspoon salt
6 slices bread, cubed
1 1/2 cups (6 oz.) shredded cheddar cheese
1 teaspoon dry mustard or 1 tablespoon prepared
    mustard
1 lb. sausage, cooked, drained, crumbled

Spray 3-quart casserole with nonstick cooking spray.

In large bowl, combine eggs, milk, salt, bread, cheese,
mustard and sausage; mix well. Pour into casserole.
Refrigerate, covered, overnight.

Heat oven to 350°F. Bake 35 to 40 minutes or until
thoroughly heated.

PICNIC PIE

MELANIE (PHIL) TATAURANGI

*This is a traditional New Zealand savory pie. Phil and I often
like to use the Christmas ham for a slightly different flavor.*

2 phyllo pastry sheets
3 cooked potatoes, sliced
5 oz. Canadian bacon, diced
1/2 onion, diced
4 eggs
1/3 cup milk
1/2 teaspoon salt
1/2 teaspoon freshly ground pepper

Heat oven to 400°F. Place one pastry sheet in 9-inch pie
pan. Place layer of potatoes in pie plate; top with layers
of bacon and onion.

Mix eggs, milk, salt and pepper; pour mixture over
potatoes and bacon.

Top with pastry sheet, crimping edges. Cut small steam
vent in top. Bake 35 minutes or until pastry has
browned. Cool 5 minutes before serving.

GREEN BEANS EVEN YOUR KIDS WILL EAT

DENA (JOHN) MAGINNES

*John and I tried desperately to teach our 18-month-old son,
Jack, to like green beans. We were without success until we made
them like this.*

2 1/2 tablespoons Dijon mustard
1/4 teaspoon salt
1/4 teaspoon freshly ground pepper
1/4 teaspoon dried tarragon
1 1/2 lb. fresh green beans, trimmed
2 teaspoons butter
3/4 cup thinly sliced shallots
2 tablespoons reduced-fat sour cream

In medium bowl, combine mustard, salt, pepper and
tarragon; set aside.

Steam green beans 5 minutes or until tender. Keep warm.

In Dutch oven, melt butter over medium heat. Add
shallots; sauté 3 minutes. Stir in mustard mixture and
green beans; toss well. Cook 2 minutes or until
thoroughly heated. Stir in sour cream; remove from heat.
Serve immediately.

VERY EASY GLAZED CARROTS

LISA (STEWART) CINK

2 tablespoons butter
2 tablespoons packed brown sugar
1 (2-lb.) bag baby carrots

In large skillet, melt butter and brown sugar over
medium heat. Add carrots; cook until desired tenderness.

AUNT IDA'S SWEET POTATO SOUFFLE

BONNIE (LARRY) MIZE

I have had this recipe since college—this was when I became turned on to the scrumptious taste of sweet potatoes. Now when I make it, I have to prepare two batches because everyone loves it so much, even the kids.

CASSEROLE

3 cups cooked mashed sweet potato

1 cup sugar

1/2 teaspoon salt

2 eggs

1/4 cup butter, melted

1/2 teaspoon vanilla

1/2 cup milk

TOPPING

1 cup packed brown sugar

1/3 cup all-purpose flour

1 cup chopped pecans

2 3/4 tablespoons butter, melted

Heat oven to 350°F.

In large bowl, combine sweet potato, sugar, salt, eggs, 1/4 cup butter, vanilla and milk; beat at medium speed until well mixed. Pour mixture into 2-quart casserole.

In medium bowl, combine brown sugar, flour, pecans and 2 3/4 cups butter; mix until well blended. Sprinkle topping over sweet potato mixture; bake, uncovered, 30 to 45 minutes or until topping is crusty and casserole is firm.

CAULIFLOWER, ONION AND CHEESE CASSEROLE

JAN (PETER) JACOBSEN

Peter and I monitor the fat content of our foods. This recipe can easily be adjusted to shave off some fat grams. Just use Pam in the casserole dish, or sauté the veggies in chicken broth.

2 tablespoons butter

1 (10-oz.) pkg. frozen cauliflower, thawed

1 onion, sliced

1/2 teaspoon salt

1/2 teaspoon freshly ground pepper

1/2 cup sour cream

1/2 cup (2 oz.) shredded Swiss cheese

1/4 cracker bread crumbs

1/4 cup (1 oz.) freshly grated Parmesan cheese

Heat oven to 350°F. Spray 1 1/2-quart casserole with nonstick cooking spray.

In medium skillet, melt butter over medium heat. Add cauliflower and onion; sauté until tender. Stir in salt, pepper, sour cream and Swiss cheese. Spoon mixture into casserole. In medium bowl, combine bread crumbs and Parmesan cheese; sprinkle over casserole.

Bake, uncovered, 30 minutes or until hot.

BROCCOLI WITH HERB BUTTER

BETH (BRAD) FABEL

This dish is delicious! It is a great variation to the usual run-of-the-mill broccoli side dish.

1 head broccoli, stems removed, leaving 1-inch from floret

1 teaspoon each fresh lemon juice, salt

1/4 cup plus 1 tablespoon butter, melted

1 tablespoon chopped fresh parsley

1/4 teaspoon salt

1 garlic clove, minced

1 tablespoon chopped fresh basil or 1/4 teaspoon dried

Steam broccoli florets 6 to 7 minutes or until slightly tender. Arrange florets in serving dish; sprinkle with lemon juice. In small bowl, combine butter, parsley, salt and garlic; mix well. Pour butter mixture evenly over broccoli.

CHICKEN-ARTICHOKE CASSEROLE

VICKY (DUFFY) WALDORF

Duffy and I enjoy having our friends over for dinner and with dinner we always have a "wine tasting". With this chicken dish, Duffy recommends Sonoma Cutrer Chardonnay. Cheers!

6 boneless skinless chicken breast
   halves
1 (10-oz.) pkg. frozen broccoli,
   thawed, drained
1 (14-oz.) can artichoke hearts,
   drained
2 (10³/₄-oz.) cans cream of
   chicken soup
1 cup mayonnaise
1/3 cup white wine
1 teaspoon fresh lemon juice
1/4 teaspoon curry powder
1/2 lb. fresh mushrooms
1/4 cup (1 oz.) grated Parmesan cheese
1 cup croutons
Hot cooked rice

Heat oven to 350°F.

In large skillet, cover chicken with water; heat over medium-high heat. Simmer 30 minutes or until chicken juices run clear. Drain and let cool. Tear meat into bite-size pieces; place in 3-quart casserole. Place vegetables on top of chicken.

In large bowl, combine soup, mayonnaise, wine, lemon juice, curry powder and mushrooms; pour over chicken and vegetables. Sprinkle with cheese. Cover with aluminum foil. Bake 40 minutes. Uncover; top with croutons. Bake an additional 15 minutes. Serve over rice.

HARVEST DISH

KATHY (CHRIS) PERRY

Chris and I love sweet potatoes, especially in the fall, so this dish is a winner at our house. It has become a part of our traditional Thanksgiving dinner.

1 cup all-purpose flour
1 cup packed brown sugar
1 cup old-fashioned or quick-cooking oats
1¹/₂ teaspoons cinnamon
²/₃ cup butter, softened
2 (16-oz.) cans yams, drained
2 cups cranberries
1¹/₂ cups miniature marshmallows

Heat oven to 350°F. Spray 1¹/₂-quart casserole with nonstick cooking spray.

In large bowl, combine 1 cup flour, brown sugar, oats and cinnamon. Toss with butter until mixture crumbles. Reserve one-third of mixture.

In another large bowl, combine yams and cranberries; spread in casserole. Top with reserved flour mixture. Bake 30 to 40 minutes or until topping is brown. Top with marshmallows. Bake until golden brown.

SONORA CASSEROLE

SHARON (DAVID) OGRIN

While at home in San Antonio, Dave and I have been known to frequent "The 410 Diner". This recipe is a take-off from a dish at that restaurant.

SAUCE
2 cups tomato sauce
1 1/2 tablespoons chili powder
1 tablespoon white vinegar
1/4 teaspoon cumin
1/4 teaspoon cayenne pepper
2 garlic cloves, minced
1/2 teaspoon salt

FILLING
1 cup vegetable oil
6 corn tortillas, cut into 1/2-inch strips
3 cups zucchini, cut into 1-inch chunks
1 cup canned corn, drained
1 (4-oz.) can green chiles, cut up
1 1/2 cups (6 oz.) shredded cheddar cheese

Heat oven to 350°F. Spray 3-quart casserole with nonstick cooking spray.

In medium saucepan, combine tomato sauce, chili powder, vinegar, cumin, cayenne, garlic and salt; simmer 1 hour. Heat vegetable oil in medium saucepan. Fry tortilla strips in oil until crisp. Drain on paper towels.

In another medium saucepan, boil or steam zucchini until tender. Combine zucchini with corn, green chiles, tortilla strips and 3/4 cup of the cheese. Spoon mixture into casserole. Cover with sauce; sprinkle remaining 3/4 cup cheese over sauce.

Bake 20 to 30 minutes or until cheese is melted. Garnish with sour cream, if desired.

SPINACH SQUARES

KATHY (CHRIS) PERRY

Kenny and I serve this as an appetizer or side dish for family gatherings and entertaining friends. It is so easy to make and always gets rave reviews.

1 cup all-purpose flour
1 cup milk
1 teaspoon salt
1 teaspoon baking powder
2 eggs, beaten
1/2 cup butter, melted
2 (10-oz.) pkg. frozen chopped spinach, thawed, drained
4 cups (16 oz.) shredded Monterey Jack cheese

Heat oven to 350°F. Spray 3-quart casserole with nonstick cooking spray; lightly flour.

Combine flour, milk, salt, baking powder, eggs and butter; stir in spinach until well mixed. Spoon mixture into casserole. Sprinkle cheese over top. Bake 30 to 40 minutes or until cheese is melted. Cut into squares and serve.

HASH BROWN CASSEROLE

CHRIS (SCOTT) GUMP

1 (2-lb.) bag frozen hash browns, thawed
1/4 cup margarine, melted
2 cups sour cream
1/2 cup chopped onion
1 (10 3/4-oz.) can cream of chicken soup
2 cups (8 oz.) shredded cheddar cheese
1 teaspoon salt
1/2 teaspoon freshly ground pepper

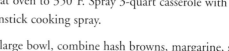

Heat oven to 350°F. Spray 3-quart casserole with nonstick cooking spray.

In large bowl, combine hash browns, margarine, sour cream, onion, soup, cheese, salt and pepper; mix well. Pour mixture into casserole. Bake, uncovered, 1 hour and 15 minutes.

FRESH MUSHROOM CASEROLE

FRAN (DILLARD) PRUITT

Our friends and family swear by this casserole. It may be the old stand-by when we have gatherings, but surely nobody complains.

1 lb. fresh mushrooms, halved
$^1/_2$ cup butter
2 beef bouillon cubes
$^1/_2$ cup hot water
2 tablespoons all-purpose flour
$^1/_2$ cup half-and-half
$^1/_8$ teaspoon salt
$^1/_8$ teaspoon freshly ground pepper
$^1/_2$ cup (2 oz.) freshly grated Parmesan cheese
$^1/_2$ cup bread crumbs

Heat oven to 350°F. Spray 1$^1/_2$-quart casserole with nonstick cooking spray.

Place mushrooms in casserole; set aside.

In medium saucepan, melt butter and bouillon in hot water. Blend in flour, half-and-half, salt and pepper. Pour mixture over mushrooms.

Combine cheese and bread crumbs; sprinkle over mushrooms. Bake, uncovered, 30 minutes.

OUR FAVORITE GREEN SALAD

PAM (DOUG) TEWELL

DRESSING
$^1/_4$ cup oil
2 tablespoons vinegar
2 tablespoons sugar
1 tablespoon chopped parsley
$^1/_2$ teaspoon salt
$^1/_2$ teaspoon freshly ground pepper
$^1/_4$ teaspoon hot pepper sauce

SALAD
$^1/_4$ head iceberg lettuce
$^1/_4$ head Romaine lettuce
1 cup chopped celery
1 (11-oz.) can mandarin oranges, drained
$^1/_4$ cup sliced almonds
1 tablespoon plus 1 teaspoon sugar

For dressing, prepare ahead so flavors can blend. In small bowl, whisk together oil, vinegar, sugar, parsley, salt, pepper and hot pepper sauce; cover and refrigerate overnight.

In large bowl, toss together lettuce, celery and oranges.

In small skillet, combine almonds and sugar. Stir constantly over low heat until sugar melts and almonds are toasted and golden brown. Cool almonds and combine with salad. Drizzle dressing over salad; toss well.

Our Favorite Green Salad

BOBOTIE

KRIS (TREVOR) DODDS

Do not let the name fool you, Trevor and I live by this dish. It is a traditional South African dish and a trip to the Southern Hemisphere would not be complete without it.

1 (3/4-inch-thick) slice bread, crusts removed, (white or wheat)

1 1/2 cups milk

2 tablespoons oil

1 tablespoon butter

2 onions, sliced

2 garlic cloves, minced

2 tablespoons curry powder

2 teaspoons salt, plus more to taste

2 tablespoons chutney

1 tablespoon smooth apricot jam

1 tablespoon Worcestershire sauce

1 teaspoon turmeric, plus more to taste

2 tablespoons vinegar

2 lb. lean ground beef

1/2 cup raisins

3 eggs

2 bay leaves

Heat oven to 300°F. Spray 3-quart casserole with nonstick cooking spray.

In large bowl, soak bread in milk. Drain and mash bread; reserve milk.

In large skillet, heat oil and butter over medium-high heat until hot. Add onions and garlic; sauté until onions are soft. Add curry powder, 2 teaspoons salt, chutney, jam, Worcestershire sauce, 1 teaspoon turmeric and vinegar; mix well. Add bread, beef and raisins. Cook over low heat, stirring occasionally, until meat is no longer pink in center. Remove from heat. Stir in 1 beaten egg. Spoon mixture into casserole.

In another large bowl, combine remaining 2 eggs and reserved milk; season with salt and turmeric. Pour over meat mixture; top with bay leaves. Place casserole in larger pan of water. Bake, uncovered, 1 hour or until set. Remove and discard bay leaves. Serve with rice, coconut, chutney, nuts and bananas, if desired.

POTATO CASSEROLE

KRIS (TREVOR) DODDS

This recipe has been served in my family as long as I can remember. It has turned into a popular dish at our house— Trevor loves it.

1/4 cup butter

1 onion, chopped

1 (2-lb.) pkg. frozen hash browns

1 (10 3/4-oz.) can cream of celery soup

1 cup reduced-fat cottage cheese

1 cup plain yogurt

2 cups (8 oz.) shredded cheddar cheese

1 cup crumbled corn flakes

Heat oven to 350°F. Spray 3-quart casserole with nonstick cooking spray.

In small skillet, melt butter over medium-high heat. Add onion; sauté 2 to 3 minutes or until tender.

In large bowl, combine hash browns, soup, cottage cheese, onion, yogurt and 1 cup of the cheddar cheese. Place mixture in casserole; top with remaining 1 cup cheddar cheese and corn flakes. Bake 45 minutes to 1 hour or until cheese is melted and browned.

PARTY POTATOES

SUE (BRAD) BRYANT

This family favorite is a great way to get the mashed potatoes done ahead of time so you aren't in the kitchen at the last minute. Plus, it stays hot for a long time—no complaints there.

12 servings instant mashed potatoes

1 cup sour cream

1 (8-oz.) pkg. cream cheese, softened

1/8 teaspoon garlic powder

1/4 cup margarine, cut into small pieces

Heat oven to 325°F. Prepare potatoes according to package directions. Spray 2-quart casserole with nonstick cooking spray.

In large bowl, combine potatoes, sour cream, cream cheese and garlic powder while potatoes are still warm; mix well. Spoon mixture into casserole; top evenly with margarine pieces. Bake, uncovered, 30 minutes.

MUSHROOM-ARTICHOKE CASSEROLE

CHRISTY (TOM) KITE

My mother passed this recipe down to me shortly after Tom and I got married. It is a favorite in our family because we both love artichokes.

3 cups sliced fresh mushrooms
$1/2$ cup chopped green onions (tops included)
4 tablespoons margarine
2 tablespoons all-purpose flour
$1/2$ teaspoon salt
$1/2$ teaspoon freshly ground pepper
$1/4$ cup milk
1 teaspoon chicken bouillon granules
1 teaspoon fresh lemon juice
$1/8$ teaspoon nutmeg
1 (10-oz.) can artichoke hearts, cooked, drained

Heat oven to 350°F. Spray 2-quart casserole with nonstick cooking spray.

In medium skillet, cook mushrooms and onion in margarine. Remove vegetables; set aside. Blend flour, salt and pepper into pan drippings. Add milk, bouillon, lemon juice and nutmeg; cook and stir until bubbly. Add mushrooms, onion and artichokes; mix well. Pour into casserole. Bake, uncovered, 20 minutes.

CHICKEN SOPA

DEBBYE (BRIAN) WATTS

This is my favorite casserole to make because it is so easy. It was given to me by Darci Todd. It comes in handy at times when you would like to help out a friend who is sick or just had a baby and cannot cook easily.

5 to 6 cooked, boneless, skinless chicken breast halves, diced
$1/2$ teaspoon salt
$1/2$ teaspoon freshly ground pepper
1 ($10^3/4$-oz.) can cream of chicken soup
1 white onion, diced
1 (14.5-oz.) can diced tomatoes and green chiles
1 (4-oz.) can green enchilada sauce
1 cup sour cream
$1/2$ cup skim milk
1 (16-oz.) pkg. 10-inch corn tortillas
2 cups (8 oz.) shredded colby-Jack cheese

Heat oven to 300°F.

In large bowl, sprinkle chicken with salt and pepper. Add soup, onion, tomatoes, enchilada sauce and sour cream. Stir in milk.

Place 1 tortilla in bottom of 13x9-inch pan. Cover tortilla with $3/4$ cup chicken mixture; sprinkle with cheese. Repeat layering, ending with tortilla. Sprinkle final layer with cheese.

Bake, uncovered, 45 minutes to 1 hour or until cheese is melted and lightly browned.

8

GORGONZOLA-SAUCED PASTA

PATTI (JOHN) INMAN

*Buff White, the TOUR Munsingwear representative, serves us
this dish when we're visiting out West.*

2 tablespoons butter
1/2 cup (2 oz.) crumbled Gorgonzola or blue cheese
1/2 to 3/4 cup heavy cream
1/8 teaspoon ground white pepper
1 (8-oz.) pkg. pasta
1/4 cup (1 oz.) freshly grated Parmesan cheese

In small saucepan, melt butter over medium-high heat.
Blend in Gorgonzola; stir in cream and white pepper.

Cook and stir about 2 minutes or until thoroughly
heated. Cook pasta according to package directions. Stir
in Parmesan cheese. Toss cheese mixture with pasta until
coated. Serve immediately.

EASY FETTUCCINE

TERRI (RICK) FEHR

*You can vary this recipe by adding chicken, salmon, crab,
shrimp or ham.*

1 (8-oz.) pkg. fettuccine
1/2 cup butter, softened
1 (8-oz.) pkg. cream cheese, softened
2 tablespoons dried parsley
2 teaspoons dried basil
2/3 cup hot water
1/2 teaspoon each freshly ground pepper, garlic salt
2 garlic cloves, minced
3/4 cup (3 oz.) freshly grated Romano or Parmesan cheese

Cook pasta according to package directions.

In medium bowl, beat 1/4 cup of the butter, cream
cheese, parsley and basil at medium speed. Add hot
water; beat thoroughly. Add pepper and garlic salt.

Transfer mixture to medium saucepan; heat over low heat.
Meanwhile, in large skillet, melt remaining 1/4 cup butter;
sauté garlic. Remove from heat; add fettuccine. Toss gently
until well coated. Transfer to serving bowl; sprinkle with
one-half of the cheese. Heat sauce, stirring constantly; pour
over fettuccine. Sprinkle remaining cheese over pasta.

SPAGHETTI NAPOLITANA

JENNIFER DE LUCA (GARY PLAYER'S DAUGHTER)

This is my dad's favorite!

1 (14.5-oz.) can tomatoes, drained, chopped
2 garlic cloves, minced
1 teaspoon chopped fresh parsley
1 tablespoon chopped fresh basil
1/4 cup olive oil
1/2 teaspoon salt
1/2 teaspoon freshly ground pepper
1 (8-oz.) pkg. spaghetti
1/4 cup (1 oz.) freshly grated Parmesan cheese

Place tomatoes in small saucepan; add garlic, parsley and
basil. Stir in olive oil, salt and pepper.

Cook sauce 15 minutes. Cook spaghetti according to
package directions. Mix pasta with sauce; top with
cheese.

CHICKEN SPAGHETTI

CINDY (BILLY RAY) BROWN

1 (8-oz.) pkg. spaghetti
1 (3- to 4-lb.) chicken
1/2 cup butter
1 large onion, chopped
1 (4-oz.) can sliced mushrooms
1 (1-lb.) loaf processed cheese spread, cubed
1 (14.5-oz.) can tomatoes

Heat oven to 375°F.

Cook spaghetti according to package directions.

In large pot, cover chicken with water. Boil chicken
about 1 hour or until tender and juices run clear.
Remove bones; cut meat into bite-size pieces.

In medium saucepan, melt butter over medium high
heat. Add onion and mushrooms; sauté until tender.
Combine spaghetti, cheese, tomatoes, onion mixture and
chicken into 2-quart casserole; mix well. Cover and bake
40 minutes. Uncover; bake an additional 10 minutes or
until brown.

RICE PILAF
BARBARA (JACK) NICKLAUS

1/2 cup butter
1/2 onion, chopped
3/4 teaspoon paprika
3/4 teaspoon dried oregano
1/2 lb. sliced fresh mushrooms
3/4 cup uncooked rice
3/4 cup water
1/2 cup sherry wine
1 (10 3/4-oz.) can beef consommé

Heat oven to 400°F.

In medium skillet, melt butter over medium heat. Add onion, paprika, oregano, mushrooms and rice; simmer 20 minutes. Place mixture into 2-quart casserole; add water, wine and consommé. Cover and bake 45 minutes. Uncover and bake an additional 15 minutes.

RICE O'BRIEN
ANNE CINK (STEWART'S MOM)

1 cup uncooked rice
2 cups water
3 chicken bouillon cubes
1 teaspoon salt
1/4 cup butter
1/2 cup sliced green onions
1/2 cup diced green bell peppers
3 tablespoons pimientos
1 (14.75-oz.) can corn
1/2 cup sliced ripe olives
1/2 teaspoon hot pepper sauce

In medium saucepan, combine rice, water, bouillon cubes and salt. Cook over medium-high until rice is tender. Set aside.

In medium skillet, heat butter until melted. Add onion and bell pepper; sauté until vegetables are crisp-tender.

Add cooked rice to skillet. Stir in pimientos, corn and olives. Season with hot pepper sauce.

LIGHTER LASAGNA
JODIE MUDD

1 1/2 lb. lean ground turkey
1/4 cup chopped fresh parsley
8 to 9 cups spaghetti sauce
8 lasagna noodles, cooked
3 1/2 cups reduced-fat ricotta cheese
1 cup chopped spinach, cooked, drained
1/4 cup (1 oz.) grated Parmesan cheese
1 tablespoon dried oregano
3/4 teaspoon nutmeg
1/2 teaspoon pepper
3 cups reduced-fat mozzarella cheese

Heat oven to 350°F. In large skillet, cook until turkey is no longer pink in center. Add parsley and sauce; cook 5 minutes.

In large bowl, mix ricotta, spinach, Parmesan, oregano, nutmeg and pepper.

Cook lasagna according to package directions.

Pour 1 cup meat sauce into 3-quart casserole; place 4 noodles on top. Place one-half of ricotta mixture over noodles. Sprinkle with 1 cup mozzarella. Repeat layers; top with remaining sauce and 1 cup mozzarella sprinkled evenly over top. Cover dish loosely with aluminum foil.

Bake 45 minutes. Remove foil; bake an additional 20 minutes. Remove from oven; let stand 10 to 15 minutes before serving.

MUSHROOM-RICE PILAF

TERRI (RICK) FEHR

Easy, and a great compliment to Aloha Pork (page 71).

1/2 cup butter
1 1/2 cups uncooked long-grain rice
1 (10 3/4 -oz.) can onion soup
1 can bouillon
1 (4-oz.) can sliced mushrooms, drained

Heat oven to 350°F. Melt butter in 2-quart casserole; stir in rice, onion soup, bouillon and mushrooms. Bake, covered, 1 hour or until rice is tender.

RESTAURANT-STYLE MARINARA

SHERI (STEVE) PATE

We often make this dish at home, and on the road for friends and family.

1/4 cup olive oil
1 medium onion, chopped
1 (32-oz.) can crushed tomatoes
4 garlic cloves, minced
2 tablespoons chopped fresh basil
1 teaspoon sugar
1/4 cup red wine
1 lb. hot or mild sausage, if desired
1 lb. fettuccine

In large skillet, heat olive oil over medium-high heat until hot. Add onion; sauté 2 minutes. Stir in tomatoes, garlic and basil. Add sugar and red wine. Simmer, covered, 15 to 20 minutes or until hot and flavorful.

Meanwhile, squeeze sausage out of casing into separate pan. Cook sausage until no longer pink in center; drain fat. Add to marinara sauce during simmer time. Serve over fettuccine.

BREAKFAST LASAGNA BY JACQUE HAMILTON (JAPAN PGA)

DEBBYE (BRIAN) WATTS

2 tablespoons vegetable oil
4 cups frozen hash browns, thawed
2 onions, chopped
8 to 10 eggs
1/2 teaspoon salt
1/2 teaspoon freshly ground pepper
1/2 cup milk
2 cups (8 oz.) shredded cheddar cheese
8 to 10 thick slices bacon, cooked, crumbled

Heat oven to 350°F. Heat oil in medium skillet over medium-high heat until hot. Add hash browns and onions; cook until hash browns are crisp, turning once. Spread into bottom of 2-quart casserole.

In large bowl, blend eggs, salt, pepper and milk; pour over cooked hash browns.

Combine cheese and bacon; sprinkle over egg mixture. Bake, covered, 40 minutes or until set.

Restaurant-style Marinara

RICE CONSOMME

CISSYE (JIM) GALLAGHER

This is easy to prepare, and a perfect companion for a holiday duck dinner (page 70).

1 onion
1/3 cup butter
1 cup uncooked rice
2 cups beef consommé
1 (8-oz.) can mushrooms

Heat oven to 375°F. Spray
3-quart casserole with nonstick cooking spray.

In large bowl, combine onion, butter, rice, consommé and mushrooms; mix well. Pour mixture into casserole. Bake, covered, 1 hour.

FETTUCCINE WITH SPINACH PESTO

KRIS (TREVOR) DODDS

1 (12-oz.) pkg. fettuccine
1/4 cup olive oil
2 tablespoons freshly chopped basil or 1 teaspoon dried
2 tablespoons Dijon mustard
2 garlic cloves, peeled
1/4 teaspoon freshly ground pepper
1/2 cup margarine, softened
1/4 cup slivered almonds
2 cups chopped fresh spinach
3/4 cup (3 oz.) freshly grated Parmesan cheese

Cook fettuccine according to package directions; drain.

Place oil, basil, mustard, garlic and pepper in blender or food processor; blend until smooth. Add margarine, almonds, spinach and cheese; blend well, scraping down sides of container after each addition. Toss with fettuccine.

TOMATO BASIL BUTTER WITH PASTA

NICOLE (MIKE) STANDLY

Mike and I first had this at the World Series of Golf in Ohio.

1 lb. pasta
1 tablespoon Dijon mustard
1/2 tablespoon Worcestershire sauce
2 sun-dried tomatoes, finely chopped
1 teaspoon fresh lemon juice
1 tablespoon minced garlic
1/2 tablespoon ground white pepper
1 tablespoon dried basil
1 teaspoon salt
1/2 cup butter

Prepare pasta according to package directions.

In large skillet, combine mustard, Worcestershire sauce, tomatoes, lemon juice, garlic, pepper, basil, salt and butter. Cook over medium-high heat until thoroughly heated. Pour mixture over pasta; toss gently.

Fettuccine with Spinach Pesto

PHOENIX OPEN PASTA

AMY (PHIL) MICKELSON

*Philip won the Phoenix Open the week I first served this dish.
I hope it's as lucky for you.*

1 lb. linguine or penne
3 tablespoons olive oil
2 garlic cloves, minced
1 (28-oz.) can tomatoes, diced, undrained
1 bunch green onions, thinly sliced
1 bunch fresh basil, chopped
4 boneless skinless chicken breast halves, cut into
   1-inch pieces
$1/8$ teaspoon salt
$1/8$ teaspoon freshly ground pepper, plus more if desired
$1/2$ cup half-and-half
1 cup fresh broccoli flowerets

Cook linguine according to package directions. Drain;
set aside.

In large saucepan, heat 1 tablespoon of the olive oil and
1 minced garlic clove over medium-high heat. Let garlic
turn slightly golden. Add tomatoes, onions and one-half
of the chopped basil. Bring mixture to a low boil.
Reduce heat; simmer 20 minutes, uncovered, until
slightly reduced.

Meanwhile, heat remaining 2 tablespoons olive oil in
heavy skillet. Add remaining garlic; do not brown. Add
chicken to skillet, sprinkle with salt and pepper. Sauté
until chicken is no longer pink in center. Set aside.

Once sauce is slightly reduced, add remaining basil and
half-and-half. Stir in chicken and broccoli. Cook until
broccoli is crisp-tender. Serve over pasta.

MEXICAN LASAGNA

DONNA (DOUG) DUNAKEY

$1^1/2$ lb. ground beef
1 (16-oz.) jar mild or medium picante sauce
$1/2$ cup water
1 (8-oz.) can tomato sauce
1 (4-oz.) can chopped green chiles, drained
2 cups (8 oz.) shredded Monterey Jack, colby or
   cheddar cheese
1 (2.8-oz.) can french fried onions
1 (12-oz.) pkg. oven-ready lasagna noodles

Heat oven to 350°F.

In large heavy skillet, cook beef until no longer pink in
center; discard fat. Stir in three-fourths of the picante
sauce, water, tomato sauce, chiles, three-fourths of the
cheese and three-fourths can of the onions; mix well.

Spray 3-quart casserole with nonstick cooking spray.
Spread remaining picante sauce in bottom of casserole.
Begin layering sauce, noodles and meat mixture; end
with meat mixture.

Bake, covered, 30 minutes. Top with remaining cheese
and onions. Bake an additional 5 minutes. Let stand 5 to
10 minutes before cutting.

9 DESSERTS

BANANA-SPLIT CHEESECAKE

JENNIFER (GLEN) RALSTON-DAY

CRUST
1³/4 cups finely crushed chocolate wafers
3 tablespoons sugar
¹/2 cup butter, melted

FILLING
3 (8-oz.) pkg. cream cheese, softened
³/4 cup sugar
5 teaspoons cornstarch
3 eggs
1 egg yolk
²/3 cup mashed banana
¹/2 cup banana schnapps
2 teaspoons vanilla

GARNISH
Pineapple
Strawberries
Chocolate syrup
Whipped cream
Chopped nuts

Heat oven to 350°F. Spray 9-inch springform pan with nonstick cooking spray. In medium bowl, combine chocolate wafers, 3 tablespoons sugar and melted butter. Press in bottom of pan.

In large bowl, beat cream cheese, ³/4 cup sugar and cornstarch at medium speed until smooth. Add eggs and egg yolk, one at a time, beating well after each addition. Beat in banana, schnapps and vanilla. Pour cream cheese mixture into crust.

Bake 15 minutes. Lower temperature to 225°F. Bake 1 hour and 10 minutes or until toothpick inserted near center comes out clean. Remove cake from oven; run knife around inside edge of pan. Turn oven off; return cake to oven an additional 30 minutes. Refrigerate, uncovered, overnight. Just before serving, garnish cheesecake with pineapple and strawberries. Drizzle with warm chocolate syrup. Add dollop of whipped cream and sprinkle with nuts.

LEMON-WHIPPED CREAM DESSERT

BYRON NELSON
I have found this dessert to be excellent over pound cake or any type of fresh fruit.

1 cup sugar
¹/2 cup fresh lemon juice
2 tablespoons grated lemon peel
3 eggs
1 cup heavy cream, whipped

In medium saucepan, combine sugar, lemon juice and lemon peel over low heat, stirring constantly until sugar dissolves. Remove from heat.

In small bowl, beat eggs at medium speed. Add a little of the hot mixture to eggs to warm; pour eggs into sugar mixture slowly, stirring constantly. Return to saucepan over low heat; cook until thickened, stirring frequently. Remove from heat; cool completely. Fold in whipped cream; refrigerate until ready to serve. Store in refrigerator.

BRANDY-APPLE TOPPING

JULIA (GLEN) HNATIUK
Glen, our daughters and I enjoyed staying at a bed and breakfast inn during one of our travels. The hospitality was great and breakfast was superb. This dish is a take-off from what we were served one morning.

¹/4 cup butter, melted
2 tablespoons brandy
1 cup golden raisins
1 cup maple syrup
¹/2 teaspoon cinnamon
¹/2 teaspoon nutmeg
2 (12-oz.) cans apple pie
    filling
1 cup roasted, skinned,
    chopped walnuts

In medium saucepan, heat and stir together butter, syrup, brandy, raisins, cinnamon, nutmeg, pie filling and walnuts. Thin with water, 1 tablespoon at a time, if necessary to make moist topping. Serve over Banana-Buttermilk Buckwheat Pancakes (page 44), or Oatmeal Pancakes (page 111).

LEMON-WHIPPED CREAM
DESSERT

SOUR CREAM COOKIES

DEBBY SCHERRER (TOM'S MOM)

1 cup butter

1 1/2 cups sugar, plus more for sprinkling

2 teaspoons vanilla

2 eggs

2 1/2 cups all-purpose flour

2 teaspoons baking powder

1 teaspoon baking soda

1 cup sour cream

1/2 cup raisins, if desired

Heat oven to 400°F. Cover several baking sheets with parchment paper.

In large bowl, beat butter, 1½ cups of the sugar and vanilla at medium speed until smooth. Beat in eggs.

In medium bowl, combine flour, baking powder and baking soda; add to butter mixture. Stir in sour cream.

Drop by teaspoonfuls onto baking sheet; sprinkle with sugar and top each with 1 raisin. Bake 7 minutes or until lightly browned.

SCHRAFFT'S CHOCOLATE SAUCE

MARY BET HORAN (TOM SHERRER'S MOTHER-IN-LAW)

1/2 cup butter

3 (1-oz.) squares unsweetened chocolate

1 cup sugar

1/8 teaspoon salt

1 cup heavy cream

1 teaspoon vanilla

In medium saucepan, melt butter, chocolate and sugar over low heat. Stir in salt and cream; cool 2 hours. Stir in vanilla. Store in refrigerator.

ORANGE CAKE

DEBBY SCHERRER (TOM'S MOM)

1 (6-oz.) can frozen orange juice concentrate, thawed

2 cups all-purpose flour

1 1/3 cups sugar

1 teaspoon baking soda

1 teaspoon salt

1/2 cup shortening

1/2 cup milk

2 eggs

1 cup raisins

1 teaspoon cinnamon

Heat oven to 350°F. Spray 9-inch round cake pan with nonstick cooking spray. In large bowl, beat 3/4 cup of the orange juice, flour, 1 cup of the sugar, baking soda, salt, shortening, milk, eggs and raisins at medium speed 3 minutes. Pour mixture into pan.

Bake 40 to 45 minutes or until toothpick inserted near center comes out clean. Cool 5 minutes on wire rack.

In small bowl, combine remaining 1/4 cup orange juice, remaining 1/3 cup sugar and 1 teaspoon cinnamon; mix well; pour over warm cake.

GIRL SCOUT GORP

PATTI (JOHN) INMAN

A Girl Scout's life can be pretty interesting, especially if you travel on the PGA TOUR. Gorp is a high energy snack food which travels well on TOUR.

2 cups salted peanuts

2 cups raisins

2 cups chopped dried apricots

2 cups candy-coated chocolate candies

4 cups bite-size shredded wheat or rice cereal

In large bowl, combine peanuts, raisins, apricots, chocolate candies and shredded wheat; toss well. Store in covered container.

OATMEAL PANCAKES

JULIA (GLEN) HNATIUK

4 cups old-fashioned or quick-cooking oats
4 cups buttermilk
7 eggs, beaten
$^1/_4$ cup sugar
$^1/_2$ cup shortening, melted
1 cup all-purpose flour
2 teaspoons baking powder
2 teaspoons baking soda
2 teaspoons salt

In large bowl, stir together oats and buttermilk. Cover and let stand, unrefrigerated, overnight.

Add eggs, sugar and shortening. Stir well to combine. Add flour, baking powder, baking soda and salt to oats mixture. Stir until just combined.

Spray griddle with nonstick cooking spray. Heat griddle to 350°F. Pour $^1/_3$ cup batter on griddle; cook until bubbles appear and underside is golden brown. Turn once. Serve with Brandy-Apple Topping (pg. 108), if desired.

DANISH APPLE DESSERT

SHIRLEY (BILLY) CASPER

Billy loves this dish after a hearty pork dinner. I enjoy baking this as much as I do eating it ... and watching everyone else indulge.

1 cup butter
1 cup plus 2 tablespoons sugar
1 teaspoon cinnamon
1 (4-oz.) pkg. rusk, crushed
4 cups heavy cream
4 cups applesauce
Sliced almonds

In medium saucepan, melt butter over low heat. Remove from heat; stir in 1 cup of the sugar and cinnamon until combined. Stir in rusk; mix until well combined.

In medium bowl, beat whipping cream at medium-high speed until stiff peaks form; gradually add remaining 2 tablespoons sugar. In 11x7x2-inch baking dish, layer rusk mixture, applesauce and whipped cream. Repeat layers, ending with cream layer. Sprinkle with almonds. Refrigerate overnight. Store in refrigerator.

CURTIS' FAMILY CHRISTMAS COOKIES

SARAH (CURTIS) STRANGE

I finally gave in and began to make only Curtis' family cookies for Christmas. It has become a family event we love to share and I even get to use his grandmother's cookie press now.

1 cup butter
1 cup sugar
1 egg
$^1/_2$ teaspoon vanilla
$2^1/_2$ cups all-purpose flour

Heat oven to 350°F. Line several baking sheets with parchment paper.

In large bowl, beat butter and sugar at medium speed until fluffy. Add egg and vanilla; beat until smooth. Mix in flour. Use cookie press to shape dough on baking sheet. Bake 10 minutes. Cool on wire rack.

WINE BARS AND GLAZE

BARBARA (JACK) NICKLAUS

BARS

1 cup butter, softened
1 1/2 cups packed brown sugar
2 eggs
1 tablespoon vanilla
4 tablespoons milk
4 tablespoons port wine
3/4 cup all-purpose flour
3/4 teaspoon baking powder
2 cups walnuts or pecans, chopped

GLAZE

2 cups powdered sugar
2 tablespoons butter
4 tablespoons port wine
1/8 teaspoon salt

Heat oven to 350°F. Spray 13x9-inch pan with nonstick cooking spray; lightly flour.

In large bowl, beat 1 cup butter and brown sugar at medium speed until fluffy. Beat in eggs. Add vanilla, milk and wine. In another large bowl, combine flour and baking powder; add to butter mixture alternately with nuts. Pour into pan. Bake 20 to 30 minutes or until lightly brown. Remove from oven; freeze 2 hours.

For glaze, in large bowl, combine powdered sugar, 2 tablespoons butter, remaining 4 tablespoons port wine and salt; beat well until smooth. Spread or drizzle glaze over bars.

LOW-FAT CHOCOLATE BISCOTTI

CHERYL (STEVE) JURGENSEN

1 1/3 cups all-purpose flour
1 cup sugar
1 tablespoon instant-coffee granules
3/4 teaspoon baking soda
1/2 teaspoon baking powder
1/4 teaspoon salt
3/4 cup chopped walnuts
1/2 cup unsweetened cocoa
1 (4-oz.) carton fat-free cholesterol-free egg product
1 teaspoon vanilla
1/4 cup sunflower oil

Heat oven to 325°F. Spray 13x9-inch pan with nonstick cooking spray.

In large bowl, mix flour, sugar, coffee granules, baking soda, baking powder and salt. Set aside.

In food processor, chop nuts. Add cocoa, egg product, vanilla and oil; pulse until moistened. Add flour mixture; pulse until moistened.

Using spatula, shape dough into log shapes 8x2 1/2 inches; arrange at least 3 inches apart in pan. Bake 35 to 48 minutes. For moist biscotti, cool slightly and slice into 1/4-inch slices; sprinkle with powdered sugar. For crunchy biscotti, slice crosswise; place cutside down on baking sheet. Bake at 300°F an additional 18 minutes. Cool completely on wire rack. Store in airtight container.

NO-BAKE CHERRY DESSERT

VICKY (DUFFY) WALDORF

This is a definite crowd pleaser! Our family loves it so much that there are never any leftovers once this dessert is placed on the table.

CRUST
36 graham-cracker squares, crushed
1/2 cup sugar
2 tablespoons butter, melted

FILLING
2 (3-oz.) pkg. cream cheese, softened
1 cup powdered sugar
2 teaspoons vanilla
2 cups frozen whipped topping, thawed
Sliced almonds

TOPPING
1 (21-oz.) can cherry pie filling
2 teaspoons almond extract

In large bowl, combine crushed crackers, sugar and butter. Press mixture in 9-inch pie plate. Set aside.

In another large bowl, combine cream cheese, powdered sugar, vanilla and whipped topping; mix until well blended. Pour mixture into crust. Top with sliced almonds.

For topping, in medium bowl, combine cherry pie filling and almond extract; mix well. Pour mixture over pie. Refrigerate until cold and firm. Store in refrigerator.

CHOCOLATE SHEET CAKE

SALLY (HALE) IRWIN

This cake is commonly made on birthdays. Hale and I love to serve it with a big scoop of vanilla ice cream.

CAKE
2 cups sugar
2 cups all-purpose flour
1 teaspoon baking soda
1 teaspoon salt
1 cup margarine
1 cup water
1/4 cup unsweetened cocoa
1/2 cup sour cream
2 eggs
1 teaspoon vanilla

FROSTING
1/2 cup margarine
1/4 cup unsweetened cocoa
6 tablespoons sour cream
1 (16-oz.) box powdered sugar
1 teaspoon vanilla

Heat oven to 350°F. Spray 15$\frac{1}{2}$x10$\frac{1}{2}$-inch pan with nonstick cooking spray.

In large bowl, combine sugar, flour, baking soda and salt. Set aside.

In medium saucepan, heat 1 cup margarine and water to boiling; remove from heat. Stir in 1/4 cup cocoa. Pour cocoa mixture over flour mixture. Stir in 1/2 cup sour cream, eggs and 1 teaspoon vanilla. Beat at medium speed until smooth. Pour into pan. Bake 15 to 20 minutes or until toothpick inserted near center comes out clean. Frost cake immediately.

Meanwhile, for frosting, heat 1/2 cup margarine, 1/4 cup cocoa and 6 tablespoons sour cream to boiling in small saucepan. Remove from heat; stir in powdered sugar and 1 teaspoon vanilla. Beat at medium speed until smooth. Spread over warm cake.

APPLE CAKE

KATHY (ROBERT) WRENN

This cake, with its rich and warm caramel sauce, is always a hit at our Thanksgiving feast. Robert requests it every year.

CAKE
1/2 cup shortening
2 cups sugar
2 eggs
2 1/2 cups all-purpose flour
2 teaspoons baking soda
1 teaspoon nutmeg
1 teaspoon cinnamon
1/2 teaspoon salt
4 cups finely chopped apples

SAUCE
1/2 cup margarine
2 tablespoons all-purpose flour
1/2 cup sugar
1/2 cup packed brown sugar
1/2 cup half-and-half

Heat oven to 375°F. Spray 9-inch round cake pan with nonstick cooking spray.

In large bowl, beat shortening, 2 cups sugar and eggs at medium speed until light and fluffy. In another large bowl, combine 2 1/2 cups flour, baking soda, nutmeg, cinnamon and salt. Add flour mixture to sugar mixture. Stir apples into batter; mix well. Pour apples into pan. Bake 30 to 45 minutes or until toothpick inserted near center comes out clean. Cool on wire rack.

For sauce, in medium saucepan, melt margarine with 2 tablespoons flour over low heat. Add 1/2 cup sugar and brown sugar; stir well. Stir in half-and-half and cook, stirring constantly, until thick. Drizzle over cake. Sprinkle with powdered sugar, if desired.

PUMPKIN DIP

TRACY (BRIAN) CLAAR

4 cups confectioner's sugar
2 (8-oz.) pkg. cream cheese, softened
1 cup canned pumpkin
2 teaspoons cinnamon
1 teaspoon ground ginger

In large bowl, combine sugar and cream cheese. Beat in pumpkin, cinnamon and ginger. Refrigerate before serving. Serve in hollowed pumpkin with ginger snaps.

Apple Cake

CARROT CAKE
SALLY (HALE) IRWIN

CAKE
1 1/2 cups vegetable oil
2 cups sugar
4 eggs
2 cups all-purpose flour
2 teaspoons baking soda
1 teaspoon salt
2 teaspoons cinnamon
3 cups grated carrots
1 cup finely chopped pecans

FROSTING
1 (8-oz.) pkg. cream cheese, softened
1/4 cup melted butter
2 teaspoons vanilla
1 (16-oz.) box powdered sugar

Heat oven to 300°F. Spray 3 (8-inch) round cake pans with nonstick cooking spray. Line bottom of pans with parchment paper.

In large bowl, beat oil and sugar at medium speed. Add eggs one at a time, beating well after each addition. In another large bowl, combine flour, baking soda, salt and cinnamon; mix well. Add to sugar mixture. Stir in carrots and nuts. Mix well. Bake 40 to 50 minutes or until toothpick inserted near center comes out clean. Cool completely in pans. Remove from pans.

To prepare frosting, in large bowl, combine cream cheese, butter, vanilla and powdered sugar; beat at medium speed until smooth. Spread over cake. Store in refrigerator.

LOW-FAT HAZLENUT BISCOTTI
CHERYL (STEVE) JURGENSEN

1 cup hazelnuts, chopped
1 cup dried cranberries, chopped
1/3 cup unsalted butter
3/4 cup sugar
1 tablespoon grated lemon peel, if desired
1 teaspoon vanilla
3 cups all-purpose flour
1 tablespoon baking powder
1 teaspoon salt
3 eggs

Heat oven to 325°F. Spray baking sheet with nonstick cooking spray.

In large bowl, combine hazelnuts, cranberries, butter, sugar, lemon peel, vanilla, flour, baking powder, salt and eggs. Shape into 2 or 3 (2 to 2 1/2-inch) rolls. Bake 15 minutes. Remove from oven; slice crosswise and place cut side down on baking sheet. Return to oven. Bake an additional 15 minutes until golden brown. Cool on wire rack. Store in airtight container.

ECLAIR CAKE
LINDA (BOBBY) WADKINS

1 (1-lb.) box graham crackers
2 (3.4-oz.) pkg. instant French vanilla pudding mix
3 1/2 cups milk
1 (8-oz.) container frozen whipped topping, thawed
1 (16-oz.) container chocolate frosting

Spray bottom of 13x9-inch pan with nonstick cooking spray. Line pan with graham crackers.

In medium bowl, mix pudding mix with milk; beat at medium speed 2 minutes. Blend in whipped topping. Pour one-half of mixture over crackers.

Place second layer of crackers over pudding mixture in pan. Repeat layers with pudding, then crackers. Refrigerate 2 hours. Spread frosting over top. Refrigerate overnight. Store in refrigerator.

SKILLET PINEAPPLE UPSIDE-DOWN CAKE

BARBARA (JACK) NICKLAUS

TOPPING
$^1/_2$ cup butter
$1^1/_4$ cups packed brown sugar
1 (20-oz.) can pineapple rings, drained

CAKE
2 eggs, separated
1 cup sugar
$^1/_4$ teaspoon vanilla
$^1/_3$ cup hot water
1 cup all-purpose flour
$1^1/_2$ teaspoons baking powder
$^1/_8$ teaspoon salt

Heat oven to 325°F.

In medium ovenproof skillet, melt butter and brown sugar over medium heat. Arrange pineapple rings over sugar mixture; cook until bubbly.

In large bowl, beat egg whites at medium speed until stiff peaks form. Increase speed to medium-high. Set aside.

In another large bowl, beat egg yolks until blended. Beat in sugar gradually; add vanilla. Add hot water and mix well. Slowly add flour, baking powder and salt. Fold in beaten egg whites. Pour batter over topping in skillet. Bake in skillet 50 minutes. Cool completely on wire rack. Invert onto cake plate; serve. Top with whipped cream, if desired.

DEANNA'S TEXAS SHEET CAKE

TRACY (BRIAN) CLAAR

When Brian and I lived in Florida, we spent a lot of time with our friends John and Suzanne Huston. This cake was always prepared before they came over because it was their absolute favorite.

CAKE
1 cup margarine
5 tablespoons unsweetened cocoa
2 cups all-purpose flour
2 cups sugar
$^1/_2$ teaspoon salt
1 teaspoon baking soda
4 eggs
$^1/_2$ cup sour cream

FROSTING
$^1/_2$ cup margarine
6 tablespoons milk
1 (16-oz.) box powdered sugar
1 teaspoon vanilla
5 tablespoons unsweetened cocoa

Heat oven to 350°F. Spray $15^1/_2$x$10^1/_2$-inch pan with nonstick cooking spray.

In small saucepan, bring 1 cup margarine and 5 tablespoons cocoa to a boil; cool.

In large bowl, combine flour, sugar, salt and baking soda. Stir in eggs and sour cream. Beat at medium speed until blended. Pour in cocoa mixture; beat at low speed until thoroughly combined.

Spread in pan. Bake 15 to 20 minutes or until toothpick inserted near center comes out clean. Cool on wire rack 5 minutes.

For frosting, in medium saucepan, melt $^1/_2$ cup margarine with milk. Heat to a boil. Remove from heat; stir in powdered sugar, vanilla and 5 tablespoons cocoa. Beat at medium speed until smooth. Spread over warm cake.

DREAM BARS

CATHI (KIRK) TRIPLETT

This is unquestionably Kirk's most requested dessert. He sometimes burns his mouth a bit when he eats these because he is too anxious to let them cool!

1 cup packed brown sugar
1 cup butter
2 cups old-fashioned or quick-cooking oats
1 1/2 cups all-purpose flour
1 teaspoon baking soda
3/4 teaspoon salt
1 cup chopped nuts
1 cup miniature candy-coated chocolate candies
1 cup semisweet chocolate chips (6 oz.)
1 (14-oz.) can sweetened condensed milk
1/4 cup peanut butter

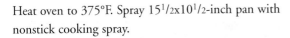

Heat oven to 375°F. Spray 15 1/2x10 1/2-inch pan with nonstick cooking spray.

In large bowl, beat brown sugar and butter at medium speed until smooth. Stir in oats, flour, baking soda, salt and nuts until mixture crumbles. Do not over mix. Press two-thirds of mixture in pan. Bake 12 minutes. Remove from oven.

In large bowl, add candies and chocolate chips to remaining one-third mixture. Toss lightly until well blended.

In small saucepan, combine sweetened condensed milk and peanut butter over low heat until smooth, stirring constantly and making sure mixture does not burn.

Pour peanut butter mixture over hot crust. Sprinkle chocolate mixture over top. Bake an additional 20 minutes or until lightly browned. Cool on wire rack.

CHOCOLATE COOKIE DESSERT

ASHLEY (HAL) SUTTON

Our family cannot get enough of chocolate cookies and ice cream. This recipe satisfies all cravings.

1 (11-oz.) pkg. chocolate wafers, crushed into crumbs
3/4 cup margarine, melted
1/2 gallon vanilla ice cream, softened
3 eggs, separated
1 1/2 cups powdered sugar
3 tablespoons unsweetened cocoa
3/4 cup salted peanuts
1 1/2 teaspoons vanilla
2 cups heavy cream

Spray 13x9-inch pan with nonstick cooking spray.

In large bowl, combine cookie crumbs and 1/4 cup of the margarine; mix until crumbly. Press two-thirds of the mixture into pan. Spread with vanilla ice cream; freeze.

In separate bowl, mix together 3 egg yolks, remaining 1/2 cup margarine, powdered sugar, cocoa, peanuts and vanilla. In medium bowl, beat egg whites at medium speed until stiff; fold into powdered sugar mixture. Pour over ice cream; freeze.

In another large bowl, whip cream until soft peaks form; spread over ice cream.

CARROT CAKE

TERRI (RICK) FEHR

Carrot cake has always been Rick's favorite. No other recipes we have tried quite live up to this one.

CAKE
2 cups sugar
1 1/2 cups vegetable oil
3 eggs
2 teaspoons vanilla
2 1/4 cups all-purpose flour
2 teaspoons cinnamon
2 teaspoons baking soda
1 teaspoon salt
2 cups shredded carrots
2 cups shredded coconut
1 (8-oz.) can crushed pineapple, drained
1 cup chopped walnuts or pecans

FROSTING
2 (3-oz.) pkg. cream cheese, softened
1/2 cup butter, melted
1/4 cup milk
2 teaspoons vanilla
1/4 teaspoon salt
3 to 4 cups powdered sugar

Heat oven to 350°F. Spray 13x9-inch pan with nonstick cooking spray.

In large bowl, combine sugar, oil, eggs and 2 teaspoons vanilla; stir with wooden spoon. Stir in flour, cinnamon, baking soda and 1 teaspoon salt. Mix well. Fold in carrots, coconut, pineapple and nuts. Pour into pan. Bake 50 minutes or until toothpick inserted near center comes out clean. Let cake cool 5 minutes; invert onto wire rack, remove pan and cool completely.

For frosting, in medium bowl, combine cream cheese, butter, milk, 2 teaspoons vanilla and 1/4 teaspoon salt. Beat at medium speed until creamy. Mix in powdered sugar; beat until smooth. Frost when cake is completely cooled. Store in refrigerator.

CHOCOLATE POUND CAKE

JULIA (GLEN) HNATIUK

This is one of our favorites. Our daughters, Aileen and Morgan, love to make this for daddy on his birthday.

6 (1.5-oz.) chocolate candy bars
2 cups sugar
1 cup butter
3/4 cup chocolate-flavored syrup
4 eggs
1 teaspoon vanilla
2 1/2 cups all-purpose flour
1 teaspoon salt
1/2 teaspoon baking soda
1 cup buttermilk

Heat oven to 350°F. Spray 12-cup Bundt pan with nonstick cooking spray.

In small saucepan over low heat, melt chocolate bars. Set aside.

In large bowl, beat sugar and butter at medium speed until fluffy; stir in chocolate syrup. Add melted chocolate; beat at low speed until thoroughly combined.

In another large bowl, stir together eggs, vanilla, flour, salt, baking soda and buttermilk. Add chocolate mixture; stir until blended. Pour into pan. Bake 1 hour. Cool in pan 20 minutes. Remove from pan; cool completely on wire rack. Sprinkle with powdered sugar or top with hot fudge, if desired.

CHOCOLATE POUND CAKE

CARROT CAKE

IRENE (GEORGE) BURNS

This cake is a favorite in our family, not only to eat but also to make. Everyone can help because, once the carrots are grated, it doesn't require much more than a bowl and a spoon.

CAKE
4 eggs
1 1/2 cups vegetable oil
2 cups sugar
2 cups all-purpose flour
1 teaspoon baking soda
1 teaspoon baking powder
1/4 teaspoon salt
2 teaspoons cinnamon
3 cups grated carrots

FROSTING
1 (8-oz.) pkg. cream cheese, softened
1/2 cup butter, softened
1 (16-oz.) box powdered sugar
1 1/2 teaspoons vanilla
1 cup chopped pecans, if desired

Heat oven to 350°F. Spray 2 (9-inch) round cake pans with nonstick cooking spray; lightly flour.

In large bowl, beat eggs and oil at medium speed. In another large bowl, mix sugar, flour, baking soda, baking powder, salt and cinnamon; mix well. Add sugar mixture to egg mixture. Add carrots; blend well. Pour mixture evenly into pans. Bake 30 to 40 minutes or until toothpick inserted near center comes out clean. Cool completely on wire rack. Remove from pans.

For frosting, beat cream cheese and butter at medium speed until fluffy. Add powdered sugar, vanilla and nuts; mix well until smooth. Spread over cake. Store in refrigerator.

PINEAPPLE DESSERT

TONI (PAUL) AZINGER

DESSERT
2 (8-oz.) cans pineapple chunks, drained
2 cups (8 oz.) shredded Cheddar cheese
2 tablespoons all-purpose flour
1 tablespoon sugar

TOPPING
2 cups graham-cracker crumbs
1/4 cup butter, melted

Heat oven to 350°F.

In large bowl, mix pineapple, cheese, flour and sugar; pour into ungreased 13x9-inch pan. Bake, uncovered, 30 minutes.

In another large bowl, combine graham-cracker crumbs and butter; sprinkle over cake. Bake, uncovered, an additional 30 minutes or until topping is browned. Garnish with whipped cream, if desired.

KAHLUA CHOCOLATE CHIP CAKE

LAURA (JOHN) FLANNERY

It is a custom in our family to prepare this cake for John on his birthday. He just can't get enough of it!

1 (18.5-oz.) box devil's food cake mix
4 eggs
1 cup sour cream
1 cup coffee-flavored liqueur
3/4 cup vegetable oil
1 cup semisweet chocolate chips (6 oz.)

Heat oven to 350°F. Spray 12-cup Bundt pan with nonstick cooking spray; lightly flour.

In large bowl, combine cake mix, eggs, sour cream, liqueur and oil; beat at low speed to blend. Increase to high speed; beat 3 to 5 minutes. Stir in chocolate chips. Pour batter into pan.

Bake 55 to 60 minutes or until toothpick inserted near center comes out clean. Cool in pan 30 minutes. Loosen cake;. invert onto wire rack. Cool completely.

OLD-FASHIONED CREAM PUFFS

ANNE CINK (STEWART'S MOM)

Take heed, these are quite time consuming, but they are more than worth it.

PASTRY
1 cup water
1/2 cup butter
1 cup all-purpose flour
4 eggs

FILLING
1/2 cup sugar
1/2 teaspoon salt
1/3 cup all-purpose flour
2 cups milk
4 egg yolks
2 teaspoons vanilla

GLAZE
1 (1-oz.) square unsweetened chocolate
1 teaspoon butter
1 cup powdered sugar
2 to 3 tablespoons boiling water

Heat oven to 400°F. Line baking sheet with parchment paper.

In medium saucepan, heat 1 cup water and 1/2 cup butter to a boil. Stir in 1 cup flour, stirring vigorously over low heat about 1 minute or until mixture leaves sides of pan and forms ball. Stir in 4 eggs, one at a time, stirring thoroughly after each addition until mixture is very smooth. Drop dough in heaping tablespoonfuls onto baking sheet about 3 inches apart. Bake 30 to 35 minutes or until puffed, golden brown and dry. Cool on wire rack.

To prepare custard filling, in large saucepan, stir together sugar, salt and 1/3 cup flour. Stir in milk. Cook over medium heat, stirring constantly, until boiling. Boil 1 minute; remove from heat. Stir one-half of hot mixture into 4 egg yolks; stir hot mixture back into pan. Heat just to a boil; cool and blend in vanilla.

To prepare glaze, in medium saucepan, melt chocolate and 1 teaspoon butter over low heat; remove from heat. Blend in powdered sugar and 2 to 3 tablespoons boiling water until glaze is smooth.

To assemble cream puffs, cut off tops of puffs; scoop out any filaments of soft dough. Fill with filling. Replace tops and frost with chocolate glaze. Store in refrigerator.

CHOCOLATE-COTTAGE CHEESE COOKIES

SUZIE (ERIC) JOHNSON

You won't believe how wonderful these cookies taste. Eric insists on making these for any guests that will be coming over.

1 cup margarine
1 cup sugar
3/4 cup packed brown sugar
2 teaspoons vanilla
2 eggs
1 cup cottage cheese
1/2 cup unsweetened cocoa
2 2/3 cups all-purpose flour
1 teaspoon baking powder
1/2 teaspoon baking soda
Powdered sugar

Heat oven to 350°F. Cover several baking sheets with parchment paper.

In large bowl, beat margarine, sugar, brown sugar, vanilla and eggs at medium speed until blended. Stir in cottage cheese; beat at low speed until combined. Stir cocoa into flour; add to margarine mixture. Stir in baking powder and baking soda. Refrigerate 30 minutes or until cold and firm.

Roll dough into golf-ball-size balls; roll in powdered sugar. Place 2 inches apart on baking sheet. Bake 10 minutes. Remove from baking sheet; cool on wire rack.

PEACH COBBLER

DIANE (FUZZY) ZOELLER

2/3 cup plus 1 tablespoon sugar
1 cup plus 2 tablespoons all-purpose flour
1/2 teaspoon cinnamon
1/2 cup plus 2 tablespoons butter, softened
3 cups sliced peaches
1 1/2 teaspoons baking powder
1/2 teaspoon salt
3 tablespoons milk
1 egg

Heat oven to 350°F. Spray 9-inch round cake pan with nonstick cooking spray.

In large bowl, combine 2/3 cup of the sugar, 2 tablespoons of the flour and cinnamon; mix well. Blend in 2 tablespoons of the butter with pastry blender or fork until mixture crumbles. Place peaches in bottom of pan; sprinkle with cinnamon mixture.

In another large bowl, combine remaining 1 tablespoon sugar, remaining 1 cup flour, remaining 1/2 cup butter, baking powder, salt, milk and egg; stir until smooth. Spoon over fruit and cinnamon mixture. Bake 30 minutes or until golden brown. Serve warm.

MINNESOURI ANGLING CLUB NO-BAKE BARS

BLAIR (MATT) GOGEL

2/3 cup white corn syrup
2/3 cup sugar
2/3 cup peanut butter
4 cups lightly toasted rice cereal
2 cups carmel chips (12 oz.)
2 cups semisweet chocolate chips (12 oz.)
1 tablespoon vegetable oil

Spray 15 1/2x10 1/2-inch pan with nonstick cooking spray. In medium bowl, bring corn syrup and sugar just to a boil. Add peanut butter. Stir well.

Measure cereal into large bowl. Pour peanut butter mixture over cereal; stir. Press in pan.

In medium saucepan, melt carmel chips, chocolate chips and oil over low heat. Spread over peanut butter and cereal mixture. Refrigerate until firm.

BANANA PUNCH

PEGGY (BOB) GILDER

Bob's mother served this beverage at our wedding rehearsal dinner in 1971. Since then it has become a big hit with children and adults for all occasions.

3 cups water
2 cups sugar
1 (46-oz.) can pineapple juice
1 1/2 cups orange juice
1/4 cup fresh lemon juice
3 bananas, mashed
3 quarts lemon-lime flavored carbonated beverage

In large pot, combine water and sugar; heat until boiling. Remove from heat; pour mixture into large plastic bowl. Stir in pineapple juice, orange juice, lemon juice and bananas; freeze overnight. Remove from freezer 20 minutes before serving. Add carbonated beverage.

PINEAPPLE CAKE

TONI (PAUL) AZINGER

CAKE
1 (18.5-oz.) box yellow cake mix
$^1/_2$ cup butter
3 eggs
$^1/_3$ cup milk
$^1/_3$ cup water
1 teaspoon vanilla

FROSTING
1 (8-oz.) can crushed pineapple
$^1/_2$ cup butter
1 cup sugar

Heat oven to 350°F. Spray 13x9-inch pan with nonstick cooking spray.

In large bowl, blend together cake mix, $^1/_2$ cup butter, eggs, milk, water and vanilla. Reserve $^3/_4$ cup batter for frosting. Bake cake according to package directions. Remove from oven. Cool thoroughly on wire rack before frosting.

For frosting, combine crushed pineapple, $^1/_2$ cup butter, sugar and reserved cake batter in medium saucepan. Cook over medium heat until mixture has thickened; cool before spreading over cake.

TINA'S COMPANY COMPOTE

TRACY (BRIAN) CLAAR

2 (8$^3/_4$-oz.) cans sliced peaches, drained overnight
2 (8$^1/_2$-oz.) cans sliced pears, drained overnight
1 (20-oz.) can pineapple chunks, drained overnight
1 (21-oz.) can cherry pie filling
$^1/_3$ cup orange-flavored liqueur
1 small bag pitted prunes (optional)

Heat oven to 350°F.

In large bowl, combine peaches, pears and pineapple (and prunes if used); mix well. Turn fruit into 3-quart casserole; top with cherry pie filling. Drizzle liqueur over top until casserole is $^2/_3$ full.

Bake 30 minutes or until bubbly.

QUICK AND EASY TOFFEE BAR CAKE

JULIE (BEN) CRENSHAW

This recipe rivals one you may find in restaurants. Ben and I love to make this simple dessert and indulge.

1 (18.5-oz.) box devil's food cake mix
1 (14-oz.) can sweetened condensed milk
1 (14-oz.) jar caramel topping
1 (8-oz.) container frozen whipped topping, thawed
2 (6-oz.) chocolate-covered English toffee candy bars, coarsely chopped

Prepare and bake cake according to package directions in 13x9-inch pan.

With end of wooden spoon, poke holes evenly every 2 inches on top of cooled cake. Pour sweetened condensed milk into holes; let soak in. Pour caramel into holes; refrigerate 4 hours.

Before serving, top with whipped topping; sprinkle with toffee bits. Store in refrigerator.

MILKTART

KRIS (TREVOR) DODDS

This dish is a very traditional South African dish, similar to custard pie. Trevor and I love it because it is so simple, yet so satisfying.

CRUST

1/2 cup butter

4 tablespoons sugar

1 egg

2 cups all-purpose flour

1/8 teaspoon salt

FILLING

2 1/2 cups milk

1 cinnamon stick

1/4 cup all-purpose flour

5 tablespoons sugar

1/8 teaspoon salt

2 tablespoons butter

3 eggs

1 teaspoon vanilla

Heat oven to 325°F.

In large bowl, cream 1/2 cup butter and 4 tablespoons sugar. Beat in 1 egg. Sift in 2 cups flour and 1/8 teaspoon salt; form into ball. Refrigerate while preparing filling.

In large saucepan, heat 2 cups of the milk and cinnamon stick over medium-high heat until hot. In small bowl, mix 1/4 cup flour, 5 tablespoons sugar and 1/8 teaspoon salt to a paste with remaining 1/2 cup milk. Stir into hot milk; cook until thick, stirring occasionally. When thick, remove from heat; add 2 tablespoons butter. Cool. Remove cinnamon stick. Beat in 3 eggs, one at a time, using wooden spoon. Add vanilla.

Press chilled dough evenly into 9-inch pie pan. Cover with parchment paper; fill with layer of dried beans. Bake 10 minutes. Remove paper and beans; bake an additional 5 minutes. Pour in filling; bake just below center of oven 20 to 25 minutes or until set. Sprinkle generously with additional cinnamon and sugar. Cool on wire rack.

CHOCOLATE CHUNK COOKIES

CAROLYN (ED) DOUGHERTY

1 1/2 cups butter, softened

1 cup packed brown sugar

1 teaspoon vanilla

1 egg

2 tablespoons honey

2 1/4 cups all-purpose flour

1 teaspoon baking soda

1 cup semisweet chocolate, coarsely chopped (6 oz.)

1 cup walnuts, chopped

Heat oven to 375°F. Spray baking sheet with nonstick cooking spray.

In large bowl, cream together butter, brown sugar and vanilla. Beat in egg and honey. Stir in flour and baking soda. Add chocolate and walnuts; mix well.

Drop mixture by teaspoonfuls 2 inches apart onto baking sheet. Bake 8 to 10 minutes or until lightly browned. Remove from baking sheet; cool on wire rack.

MARY'S FROSTED ORANGE

BONNIE (LARRY) MIZE

This recipe is the closest thing that Larry and I have ever tasted to a commercial orange slush beverage. It is much more fun to make it on our own … and the labor isn't intense at all.

1 (6-oz.) can frozen orange juice concentrate, thawed

1/2 cup sugar

1 cup water

1 cup milk

1/2 teaspoon vanilla

Ice cubes

In blender, combine juice concentrate, sugar, water, milk and vanilla. Add ice cubes to fill blender. Blend until ice is crushed. Serve immediately. Store in freezer.

MOLASSES SUGAR COOKIES
DEBBY SCHERRER (TOM'S MOM)

3/4 cup shortening
1 1/2 cups sugar
1/4 cup molasses
1 egg
2 teaspoons baking soda
2 cups all-purpose flour
1/2 teaspoon ground cloves
1/2 teaspoon ground ginger
1/2 teaspoon nutmeg
1 teaspoon cinnamon
1/2 teaspoon salt

Heat oven to 375°F. Line several baking sheets with parchment paper.

In large bowl, combine shortening, 1 cup of the sugar, molasses, egg, baking soda, flour, cloves, ginger, nutmeg, cinnamon and salt; mix until thoroughly combined.

Roll mixture into 1-inch dough balls.

Place remaining 1/2 cup sugar in medium resealable plastic bag. Shake dough balls, one at a time, in bag. Place 2 inches apart on baking sheet.

Bake 10 minutes. Cool on wire rack.

SPECIAL OATMEAL COOKIES
TERRI (RICK) FEHR

I baked and sold these cookies at a golf course where I worked when I was in high school. They were a hit then and golfers still love them.

2 cups sugar
1 cup shortening
2 eggs
2 tablespoons molasses
1 1/2 teaspoons salt
1 1/2 teaspoons baking soda
2 teaspoons vanilla
2 teaspoons cinnamon
2 cups all-purpose flour
2 cups old-fashioned or quick-cooking oats
2/3 cup raisins
2/3 cup dates
2/3 cup chopped pecans or walnuts

Heat oven to 375°F. Spray baking sheet with nonstick cooking spray.

In large bowl, beat sugar, shortening and eggs at medium speed until creamy. Blend in molasses, salt, baking soda, vanilla and cinnamon. Gradually beat in flour. Stir in oats, raisins, dates and nuts until thoroughly mixed.

To form cookies, lightly press dough into ice-cream scoop; level off. Place dough balls 2 inches apart, flat side down onto baking sheet. Bake 10 minutes. Remove from baking sheet; cool on wire rack.

MOLASSES SUGAR COOKIES

PUMPKIN MOUSSE DREAM PIE

SHIRLEY (BILLY) CASPER

One of the highlights of the Billy Casper family holiday celebration is my pumpkin pie. Best to serve small portions— this pie is extremely rich.

2 (8-oz.) pkg. cream cheese, softened
$1/4$ cup canned pumpkin
$1/4$ teaspoon nutmeg
$1/4$ teaspoon ground cloves
1 teaspoon cinnamon
1 (8-oz.) container frozen whipped topping, thawed
$1 1/2$ cups powdered sugar
$1 1/2$ teaspoons vanilla
1 (9-inch) graham-cracker pie shell

In large bowl, beat cream cheese until smooth. Add pumpkin and spices; mix well. Reserve 1 cup whipped topping; add remaining topping and mix well. Add powdered sugar and vanilla; whip until blended.

Pour into shell; top with reserved topping. Refrigerate 2 hours. Store in refrigerator.

Pumpkin Mousse Dream Pie

FRESH APPLE CAKE

ELAYNA (STAN) UTLEY

No time is better for this cake than a brisk autumn day. Stan and I love to bake this cake and eat it on the porch, looking at the changing leaves.

1 cup vegetable oil
2 eggs
2 cups sugar
1 teaspoon vanilla
3 cups chopped apples
1 cup chopped nuts
3 cups all-purpose flour
1 teaspoon salt
1 teaspoon baking soda
1 teaspoon cinnamon

Heat oven to 300°F. Spray 9-inch round cake pan with nonstick cooking spray.

In medium bowl, combine oil, eggs, sugar and vanilla; mix well. Slowly stir in apples, nuts, flour, salt, baking soda and cinnamon.

Pour mixture into pan. Bake 1 hour. Serve warm with ice cream or whipped topping.

MOTHER'S COBBLER

BONNIE (LARRY) MIZE

My father loved to fish and after every fish fry my mother would make this cobbler and serve it with ice cream. Larry has learned to love it as much as I do.

1/2 cup butter
1 cup sugar
1 cup self-rising flour
1 cup milk
1 1/2 cups fresh fruit

Heat oven to 350°F. Place butter in 2-quart casserole; place casserole in oven to melt butter. Remove casserole from oven.

In medium bowl, combine sugar, flour and milk. Pour mixture into casserole. Top with fruit. Bake 1 hour or until fruit is bubbly and crust is lightly browned. Cool 10 minutes. Serve warm.

CREAM CHEESE CUPCAKES

CHRIS (SCOTT) GUMP

This recipe was given to me by my mother and is Scott's favorite dessert. No matter who makes it, he'll eat them right up.

1 (18.5-oz.) box chocolate cake mix
1 (8-oz.) pkg. cream cheese, softened
1/2 cup sugar
1 egg
Dash salt
1 cup miniature semisweet chocolate chips (6 oz.)

Heat oven to 350°F. Spray muffin cups with nonstick cooking spray. Place paper baking cup in each cup. Prepare cake according to package directions. Fill paper baking cups two-thirds full of batter, reserving some batter for tops.

In medium bowl, beat together cream cheese and sugar at medium speed until combined. Add egg and salt; mix again. Stir in chocolate chips. Drop 1 teaspoon of cheese mixture into each cup; top with remaining cake batter.

Bake 20 to 25 minutes. Cool on wire rack.

MOTHER'S BANANA CREAM PIE

BONNIE (LARRY) MIZE

My mother has made this recipe since 1944. It definitely stands the test of time—Larry and I make it often for special occasions, despite the time it may take to prepare. It is worth it!

3 egg yolks, slightly beaten
1/3 cup all-purpose flour
2/3 cup sugar
1/4 teaspoon salt
2 cups milk
2 tablespoons butter
1/2 teaspoon vanilla
4 to 6 ripe bananas, sliced
1 (9-inch) baked pie shell
Heavy cream, whipped

Place egg yolks in medium bowl; set aside.

In medium saucepan, whisk together flour, sugar, salt and milk over medium heat. Cook until mixture has thickened, stirring constantly. When thickened, slowly pour flour mixture into beaten egg; return flour-egg mixture to saucepan. Cook over low heat 2 minutes; remove from heat. Cool 30 minutes. Stir in butter and vanilla. Fold in bananas. Pour into pie shell. Refrigerate 5 hours or until set. Top with whipped cream.

BARBARA'S CHEESECAKE

BARBARA (JACK) NICKLAUS

CRUST

1^1/$_2$ cups graham-cracker crumbs

2 tablespoons sugar

1 teaspoon all-purpose flour

^{1}/$_4$ cup butter, melted

FILLING

4 cups cream cheese, softened

1 cup sugar

2 eggs

2 teaspoons vanilla

TOPPING

2 cups sour cream

^{3}/$_4$ cup sugar

^{3}/$_4$ teaspoon vanilla

^{1}/$_2$ teaspoon fresh lemon juice

Heat oven to 350°F.

In medium bowl, combine graham-cracker crumbs, 2 tablespoons sugar, flour and butter. Press in 10-inch springform pan. Bake 10 minutes. Remove from oven; cool.

To prepare filling, in another medium bowl, combine cream cheese, 1 cup sugar, eggs and 2 teaspoons vanilla. Pour over cooled crust. Bake 30 minutes.

To prepare topping, in another bowl, combine sour cream, ^{3}/$_4$ cup sugar, ^{3}/$_4$ teaspoon vanilla and lemon juice. Spread over cheesecake. Return to oven; bake an additional 8 minutes. Cool on wire rack. Refrigerate overnight. Store in refrigerator.

RUM CAKE

SHARON (DAVID) OGRIN

This cake gets better and better with age. David and I have been enjoying it for years now and never tire of it.

CAKE

1 (18.5-oz.) box yellow cake mix

^{1}/$_2$ cup rum

^{1}/$_2$ cup water

1 (3.4-oz.) pkg. instant vanilla pudding mix

^{1}/$_2$ cup oil

4 eggs

GLAZE

^{1}/$_4$ cup water

1 cup sugar

^{1}/$_2$ cup butter

^{1}/$_4$ cup rum

Heat oven to 325°F. Spray 12-cup Bundt pan with nonstick cooking spray; lightly flour.

In large bowl, combine cake mix, ^{1}/$_2$ cup rum, ^{1}/$_2$ cup water, pudding mix and oil; beat at medium speed until smooth. Beat in eggs one at a time. Pour mixture into pan. Bake 1 hour. Leave cake in pan on wire rack to cool.

In medium saucepan, combine ^{1}/$_4$ cup water, sugar and butter; bring to a boil. Let cool 10 minutes. Add ^{1}/$_4$ cup rum. Poke holes in cake with wooden spoon handle or ice pick. Pour glaze slowly over cake, filling holes. When completely cool, remove cake from pan.

MARGARITA PIE

SHARON (DAVID) OGRIN

CRUST
6 tablespoons butter, melted
3/4 cup crushed salted pretzels
1/2 cup sugar

FILLING
3/4 cup heavy cream
1 (14-oz.) can sweetened condensed milk
3 tablespoons fresh lime juice
1 drop green food color
1 1/2 tablespoons Tequila
1 1/2 tablespoons orange-flavored liqueur
Lime slices

In large bowl, combine butter, pretzels and sugar; mix until well blended. Press mixture in 10-inch springform pan. Set aside.

In another bowl, beat whipping cream on high speed until stiff. Gently fold in sweetened condensed milk, lime juice and food color.

Add tequila and triple sec; mix well. Pour mixture over crust. Freeze 24 hours. Serve frozen. Garnish with lime slices.

CHOCOLATE MOUSSE

CATHI (KIRK) TRIPLETT

This dessert was served to Kirk and me during our first stay in Scotland for the British Open at Turnberry. It tastes like heaven!

1 lb. semisweet chocolate
1/4 cup rum or brandy
6 pasteurized eggs, separated
1 cup heavy cream

Break chocolate into squares. In medium microwave-safe bowl, combine chocolate and rum; microwave on High power 2 1/2 minutes. Stir until smooth. In small bowl, beat egg yolks; stir into chocolate mixture.

In large bowl, beat cream at high speed until soft peaks form; fold into chocolate mixture. In another bowl, beat egg whites until stiff peaks form; fold into chocolate mixture. Turn chocolate mixture into 9-inch pie pan. Refrigerate several hours or overnight. Sprinkle chocolate shavings over mousse, if desired.

PETTICOAT TAILS (SHORTBREAD COOKIES)

CATHI (KIRK) TRIPLETT

Kirk and I have fabulous neighbors in Nashville. They have spoiled us rotten with their fabulous cooking. I stole this recipe from them so that Kirk and I can return the hospitality.

1 lb. butter, softened
1 cup sugar
5 cups all-purpose flour
1 teaspoon vanilla

In large bowl, beat butter and sugar at medium speed until fluffy. Add flour and vanilla; beat until smooth. Form mixture into rolls 1 1/4 inches in diameter. Wrap rolls in parchment paper; freeze overnight.

Heat oven to 350°F. Allow rolls to partially thaw; slice into 1/8-inch slices. Arrange slices 2 inches apart on ungreased baking sheet. Bake until just brown along edges. Remove from baking sheet. Cool on wire rack.

PEANUT BUTTER COOKIES

CATHI (KIRK) TRIPLETT

This is a great recipe for any old rainy afternoon. Kirk thinks this beats any standard peanut butter cookie recipe.

$1/2$ cup sugar
$1/2$ cup packed brown sugar
$1/2$ cup butter, softened
$1/2$ cup peanut butter
2 tablespoons milk
1 teaspoon vanilla
1 egg
$1 3/4$ cups all-purpose flour
1 teaspoon baking soda
$1/2$ teaspoon salt

Heat oven to 375°F.

In large bowl, combine sugar, brown sugar and butter; beat at high speed until smooth. Stir in peanut butter, milk, vanilla and egg; blend well. Stir in flour, baking soda and salt.

Shape dough into 1-inch balls; roll in sugar. Arrange balls 2 inches apart on ungreased baking sheet. Flatten in crisscross pattern with fork. Bake 10 to 12 minutes or until golden brown. Remove cookies from baking sheet. Cool on wire rack.

BLACK AND WHITE COOKIES

CATHI (KIRK) TRIPLETT

Kirk and I will eat chocolate chip cookies until we are sick! This recipe is on our all-time best recipe list.

$2 1/4$ cups all-purpose flour
$1/2$ cup unsweetened cocoa
$1/2$ teaspoon baking soda
$1/4$ teaspoon salt
1 cup packed brown sugar
$3/4$ cup sugar
1 cup butter, softened
3 eggs
2 teaspoons vanilla
1 cup semisweet chocolate, coarsely chopped
1 cup white chocolate, coarsely chopped

Heat oven to 300°F.

In medium bowl, combine flour, cocoa, baking soda and salt; mix well with wire whisk. Set aside.

In large bowl, beat sugars at medium speed. Add butter and mix to form grainy paste, scraping down sides of bowl. Add eggs and vanilla. Beat at medium speed until smooth.

Add flour mixture and chocolate chunks. Blend at low speed until just combined. Do not over mix.

Drop mixture by rounded tablespoonfuls $2 1/2$ inches apart onto ungreased baking sheet. Bake 23 to 25 minutes. Remove from baking sheet. Cool on wire rack.

JAN SMUTS' TEA CAKES

MRS. J. COLE (BOBBY'S MOM)

3/4 cup butter
1 1/2 cups plus 2 tablespoons all-purpose flour
3/4 cup sugar
1/8 teaspoon salt
1 1/2 teaspoons baking powder
2 eggs, beaten
2 to 3 tablespoons milk
Jam

Spray 1 3/4-inch muffin cups with nonstick cooking spray.

In large bowl, work 1/2 cup of the butter into 1 1/2 cups flour using pastry blender or two knives until mixture crumbles. Add 1/2 cup of the sugar, salt, 1 teaspoon of the baking powder and 1 egg. Gradually add milk until mixture forms ball. Refrigerate 30 minutes. Roll out on floured surface until 1/4 inch thick. Cut to fit in bottom and up sides of muffin cups.

Heat oven to 425°F. In medium bowl, beat remaining 1/4 cup butter and remaining 1/4 cup sugar at medium speed until fluffy. Add remaining egg. Beat in remaining 2 tablespoons flour and remaining 1/2 teaspoon baking powder; mix well. Place 1 teaspoonful jam in each tart. Drop 1 teaspoon butter mixture on top of jam. Bake 12 to 15 minutes or until light brown. Let cool slightly on wire rack before removing from muffin cups.

MAX'S FAVORITE DIRT CUPS

COURTNEY (BILL) GLASSON

1 (3.4-oz.) pkg. instant chocolate pudding mix
4 (9-oz.) clear plastic drinking cups
1 cup crushed chocolate wafers
1 package gummy worms candy

Prepare pudding according to package directions.

Spoon 1/2 cup of pudding into each plastic cup. Pudding can be mixed with some crushed cookies, if desired. Spoon about 1/2 inch crushed cookies on top of pudding. Use straw to make holes for worms; insert worms into holes so worms partially extend over rim of cup. Store in refrigerator.

Jan Smuts' Tea Cakes

PUMPKIN PIE

CATHI (KIRK) TRIPLETT

1³/₄ cups milk
2 eggs
1³/₄ cups canned pumpkin
2 tablespoons molasses
¹/₂ teaspoon salt
²/₃ cup packed brown sugar
2 tablespoons sugar
1¹/₄ teaspoons cinnamon
¹/₂ teaspoon ground ginger
¹/₂ teaspoon nutmeg
¹/₄ teaspoon ground cloves
1 (9-inch) unbaked pie shell

Heat oven to 425°F.

In small bowl, combine milk and eggs; mix well. In large bowl, combine pumpkin, molasses, salt, brown sugar, sugar, cinnamon, ginger, nutmeg and cloves; mix well. Gradually stir in milk and eggs.

Pour mixture into pie shell. Bake 45 to 60 minutes or until toothpick inserted near center comes out clean. Cool on wire rack.

CHOCOLATE-PEANUT CLUSTER CANDIES

SUE (BRAD) BRYANT

2 cups semisweet chocolate chips (12 oz.)
2 cups butterscotch chips (12 oz.)
2 tablespoons peanut butter
2 cups salted Spanish peanuts

In medium microwave-safe bowl, combine chips and peanut butter; cover with plastic wrap. Microwave on High 4 minutes; stir until melted. Stir in peanuts. Drop by teaspoonfuls onto parchment paper or into 1-inch candy cups. Cool until firm before serving.

STRAWBERRY-RHUBARB PIE

CATHI (KIRK) TRIPLETT

This recipe comes from the best pie-baker around ... my mother. She had a lot of practice feeding her "sweet-craving" clan when I was younger. Now I enjoy serving my own sweets-lovers!

CRUST
2 cups all-purpose flour
1 teaspoon salt
²/₃ cup plus 2 tablespoons shortening
5 to 7 tablespoons ice water

FILLING
1¹/₂ cups sugar
¹/₄ cup all-purpose flour
2 cups cleaned sliced strawberries
2 cups cleaned chopped rhubarb
Butter

Heat oven to 450°F.

In medium bowl, combine 2 cups flour and salt. Cut in shortening using pastry blender or fork until mixture crumbles. Sprinkle flour mixture with water, 1 tablespoon at a time. Mix lightly with fork until dough is just moist enough to hold together. Divide dough into two balls; refrigerate.

To prepare filling, in another bowl, combine sugar and ¹/₄ cup flour. Gently stir in strawberries and rhubarb. Set aside.

Removed chilled pastry; roll each ball into pastry round. Using parchment paper, dust both paper and dough with flour to prevent sticking. Roll each pastry round into circle at least 10 inches in diameter.

Carefully place one pastry crust in bottom of 9-inch pie plate, pressing firmly into place. Pour filling into crust. Dot with small pieces of butter. Cover with remaining crust. Seal edges with water; pinch crust together, trimming excess. Cut slits in top crust for steam to escape.

Bake 40 to 45 minutes or until juice bubbles through crust. Cool on wire rack.

BRER RABBIT MOLASSES COOKIES

KATHY (ROBERT) WRENN

I have found the truth in the saying "the best way to a man's heart is through his stomach". These cookies bring a warm smile to my husband's face—in between bites that is.

3/4 cup shortening
1 1/4 cups sugar
1/4 cup molasses
1 egg
2 cups all-purpose flour
1/2 teaspoon ground cloves
1/2 teaspoon ground ginger
1 teaspoon cinnamon
2 teaspoons baking soda
1/2 teaspoon salt

Heat oven to 375°F. Spray baking sheet with nonstick cooking spray.

In large saucepan, melt shortening over low heat; cool. Add 1 cup of the sugar, molasses and egg; beat together well. Sift flour, cloves, ginger, cinnamon, baking soda and salt into saucepan; mix well. Remove from heat; refrigerate at least 2 hours.

Form mixture into 1-inch balls; roll in remaining 1/4 cup sugar. Place balls 2 inches apart on baking sheet. Bake 8 to 10 minutes or until browned at edges and slightly firm. Remove from baking sheet. Cool on wire rack.

SALLY'S CARROT CAKE

SALLY (SCOTT) HOCH

CAKE
2 cups all-purpose flour
2 teaspoons baking powder
1 1/2 teaspoons baking soda
1 teaspoon salt
2 teaspoons cinnamon
2 cups sugar
1 1/2 cups vegetable oil
4 eggs
2 cups grated carrots
1 (8 1/4-oz.) can crushed pineapple, drained
1/2 cup chopped pecans or walnuts

FROSTING
1/2 cup butter, softened
1 (8-oz.) pkg. cream cheese, softened
1 teaspoon vanilla
1 (16-oz.) box powdered sugar

Heat oven to 350°F. Spray 8-inch square pan with nonstick cooking spray.

In large bowl, sift together flour, baking powder, baking soda, salt and cinnamon. Add sugar, oil and eggs; mix well. Stir in carrots, pineapple and nuts until well blended. Pour into pan. Bake 45 minutes or until toothpick inserted near center comes out clean. Cool cake in pan.

To prepare frosting, in large bowl, combine butter, cream cheese and vanilla; mix well. Beat in powdered sugar at high speed until smooth. Spread over cake.

JUICY LEMON CAKE

JUDY (MIKE) BRISKY

This cake is a staple at any holiday celebration or family gathering. Mike and I look forward to sharing this recipe with generations to come.

4 eggs
3/4 cup vegetable oil
1 (3.4-oz.) pkg. instant lemon pudding mix
1 cup water
1/2 cup plus 2 teaspoons fresh lemon juice
1 teaspoon lemon extract
1 (18.5-oz.) box lemon supreme cake mix
1 teaspoon grated lemon peel
1 1/2 cups powdered sugar

Heat oven to 350°F. Spray 12-cup Bundt pan with nonstick cooking spray.

In large bowl, beat eggs, oil, pudding mix and water at medium speed. Stir in 2 teaspoons of the lemon juice, lemon extract, cake mix and lemon peel; beat until smooth. Pour mixture into pan. Bake 40 minutes. Cool on wire rack 10 minutes. Remove from pan; transfer to cake platter.

Meanwhile, combine remaining 1/2 cup lemon juice and powdered sugar; mix together until smooth. Pour glaze over warm cake.

COLA CHOCOLATE CAKE

JENNIFER (GLEN) RALSTON-DAY

CAKE
4 cups all-purpose flour
8 tablespoons cocoa
1 tablespoon cinnamon
2 teaspoons baking soda
1 teaspoon salt
1 lb. butter
4 eggs
1 cup buttermilk
4 teaspoons vanilla
2 cups cola
4 cups sugar

ICING
1/2 cup butter
1/2 cup cola
6 tablespoons cocoa
1 cup chopped pecans
2 teaspoons vanilla
2 (16-oz.) boxes powdered sugar

Heat oven to 350°F. Spray 11x17-inch pan with nonstick cooking spray.

In large bowl, sift together flour, 1/2 cup cocoa, cinnamon, baking soda and salt; set aside. In medium saucepan, heat 1 lb. butter and 2 cups cola until butter has melted. Add eggs, 4 teaspoons vanilla and buttermilk; mix well. Add liquid to flour mixture; beat at high speed until smooth. Pour mixture into pan.

Bake 30 minutes.

To prepare icing, in medium bowl, combine 1/2 cup butter, 1/2 cup cola, 6 tablespoons cocoa, pecans, 2 teaspoons vanilla and powdered sugar. Beat at high speed until smooth. Spread over warm cake.

OREO DESSERT

RYNDEE (MICHAEL) CLARK

1 (15-oz.) pkg. oreo cookies
$^1/_2$ cup butter, melted
$^1/_2$ gallon vanilla ice cream, softened
1 (4-oz.) chocolate bar
$^2/_3$ cup sugar
1 (5-oz.) can evaporated milk
1 teaspoon vanilla
$^1/_2$ teaspoon salt
1 (8-oz.) container frozen whipped topping, thawed

With rolling pin, crush cookies in large resealable plastic bag. In large bowl, combine cookie crumbs and butter; mix well.

Spread mixture in 9-inch round cake pan. Spread soft ice cream evenly on top; freeze.

In small saucepan, combine chocolate bar, sugar, milk, vanilla and salt; boil 4 minutes. Cool 10 minutes. Pour evenly over ice cream. Freeze another 20 minutes until firm. Top with whipped cream. Freeze until ready to serve.

PECAN PIE

SALLY (HALE) IRWIN

3 eggs, beaten
$^1/_2$ cup sugar
$^1/_8$ teaspoon salt
1 teaspoon vanilla
3 tablespoons butter, melted
1 cup dark corn syrup
$1^1/_3$ cups pecan halves
1 (9-inch) unbaked pie shell

Heat oven to 350°F.

In large bowl, combine eggs, sugar, salt, vanilla, butter and corn syrup; mix well. Stir in pecans; pour into pie shell. Bake 30 minutes or until set. Cool on wire rack. Top with whipped cream, if desired.

MOLASSES CRINKLES

TERRI (RICK) FEHR

These are my all-time favorite cookies—crunchy on the outside and chewy on the inside. Can't get much better than that!

$^3/_4$ cup butter, softened
1 cup sugar
$^1/_4$ cup molasses
1 egg
$2^1/_4$ cups all-purpose flour
2 teaspoons baking soda
$1^1/_2$ teaspoons ground ginger
1 teaspoon cinnamon
$^1/_2$ teaspoon ground cloves
$^1/_2$ teaspoon salt

Heat oven to 375°F. Spray baking sheet with nonstick cooking spray.

In medium bowl, beat butter and sugar at medium speed 5 to 8 minutes or until light and fluffy. Beat in molasses and egg until blended. Sift flour, baking soda, ginger, cinnamon, cloves and salt into mixture. Stir with wooden spoon to make stiff dough.

Shape dough into walnut-size balls; roll in sugar to coat. Place cookie dough about $2^1/_2$ inches apart on baking sheet.

Bake 12 to 14 minutes. Remove cookies from baking sheet; cool on wire rack.

PATRICIA ROLLINS' CINNAMON CAKE

JENNY (JOHN) ROLLINS

This is John's mom's special recipe. John asked me to bake this for him when we were in college—it was actually a test to decide whether I was a keeper or not! Turns out, with the help of this magnificent recipe, I was!

CAKE
1 (18.5-oz.) box yellow cake mix
1 (3.4-oz.) pkg. instant vanilla pudding mix
4 eggs
3/4 cup water
1 teaspoon vanilla
1 teaspoon butter
1/2 cup sugar
1/2 cup packed brown sugar
2 tablespoons cinnamon
1/2 cup pecans

GLAZE
1 cup powdered sugar
3 tablespoons milk
1 teaspoon vanilla
1 teaspoon butter

Heat oven to 325°F. Spray 12-cup Bundt pan with nonstick cooking spray.

In large bowl, beat cake mix, pudding, eggs, water, 1 teaspoon vanilla and 1 teaspoon butter at high speed 8 minutes or until soft peaks form. In medium bowl, combine sugar, brown sugar, cinnamon and pecans; mix well.

Sprinkle some sugar mixture on bottom of pan. Add thin layer of batter followed by layer of sugar mixture. Finish with heavy layer of batter and remaining layer of sugar mixture. Swirl with knife.

Bake 60 to 70 minutes. Leave in pan 10 minutes. Invert onto serving platter.

To prepare glaze, in medium bowl, combine powdered sugar, milk, 1 teaspoon vanilla and 1 teaspoon butter; mix well. Pour glaze over top of warm cake.

POPPY-SEED CAKE

JAN (PETER) JACOBSEN

This cake is remarkable! Peter and I won a March of Dimes celebrity cooking contest using this recipe, and our kids even choose this cake over ones with frosting on them!

1 teaspoon sugar
1 teaspoon cinnamon
4 eggs
1 teaspoon almond extract
1/4 cup poppy seeds
1/4 cup rum
1/2 cup pineapple juice
1/2 cup vegetable oil
1 (18.5-oz.) box white cake mix
1 (3.4-oz.) pkg. instant vanilla pudding mix

Heat oven to 350°F. Spray 12-cup Bundt pan with nonstick cooking spray; sprinkle with sugar and cinnamon.

In large bowl, beat eggs, almond extract, poppy seeds, rum, pineapple juice and oil at medium speed until well mixed. Stir in cake mix and pudding mix; beat at medium speed until well combined. Pour batter into pan.

Bake 50 to 55 minutes or until toothpick inserted near center comes out clean. Cool on wire rack. Invert onto serving platter; lightly dust with powdered sugar, if desired.

INDEX